michael slaughter

momentum for life

workbook

Biblical Principles for Sustaining
Physical Health, Personal Integrity, and Strategic Focus

ABINGDON PRESS
NASHVILLE

MOMENTUM FOR LIFE:
BIBLICAL PRINCIPLES FOR SUSTAINING PHYSICAL HEALTH,
PERSONAL INTEGRITY, AND STRATEGIC FOCUS—WORKBOOK

Copyright © 2008 Michael Slaughter

All rights reserved.

ISBN 978-0-687-65303-4

08 09 10 11 12—5 4 3 2 1
MANUFACTURED IN THE UNITED STATES OF AMERICA

contents

before you begin

In the journey of life and faith, most good things don't happen magically or suddenly. They are the result of a predetermined desire, an ongoing commitment to work toward the desired goal or outcome. What keeps us moving forward? *Momentum.*

The apostle Paul compares the life of faith to running a race that requires the impetus of momentum:

> *Do you not know that in a race all the runners run, but only one gets the prize? Run in such a way as to get the prize. Everyone who competes in the games goes into strict training. They do it to get a crown that will not last, but we do it to get a crown that will last forever. Therefore I do not run like someone running aimlessly; I do not fight like a boxer beating the air. No, I strike a blow to my body and make it my slave so that after I have preached to others, I myself will not be disqualified for the prize.* (1 Corinthians 9:24-27)

Is *your* life characterized by momentum? Are you moving toward your God-given dreams and destiny despite the obstacles and challenges? This study will help you to do just that by building momentum for life—momentum that will keep you moving toward God's promised future in every major area of your life: spiritual, intellectual, interpersonal, vocational/missional, and physical. The study focuses on key practices for these areas of your life based on the acronym D-R-I-V-E:

Devotion to God
Readiness for Lifelong Learning
Investing in Key Relationships
Visioning for the Future
Eating and Exercise

After an introductory session (Week 1), each of the following five sessions (Weeks 2-6) is devoted to one of the practices of D-R-I-V-E. You will explore ways to:

- increase your passion for God and be fully present to God's presence each day
- stretch your mind so that your work will be more creative, innovative, excellent, and redemptive
- invest in key relationships and make a difference in the lives of others
- envision and move toward God's purpose and direction for your future, persevering despite opposition and resistance
- make a disciplined commitment to healthy eating and exercise habits

As you begin this exciting journey to build momentum in every area of your life, be encouraged by the fact that you do not travel alone. Throughout your journey, you and the other members of your group will pray for one another, encourage one another, and hold one another accountable. Each week in your group session you will have the opportunity to connect with one another, pray together, watch a brief video, discuss your insights and learnings, and share how you plan to respond.

Prior to each group session, be sure to complete all of the questions provided for personal reflection—those within the lesson (printed in bold) as well as those at the end (Momentum Builders). You will be invited to share your responses to some of these questions during the group session.

As you begin to apply what you are learning and follow through with specific action steps, take advantage of the opportunity to give and receive accountability and encouragement with other members of your group. Depending upon the size of your group, you may choose to assign accountability partners or small groups who can exchange e-mail addresses for quick and easy communication during the week. May the camaraderie you develop during these six weeks extend well beyond the study, providing ongoing fellowship and support for your continued pursuit of momentum for life!

Week 1
Momentum: Mass in Motion

Mass in motion. Quantity of forward motion. Impetus. i.e.: "A team that has momentum is on the move and hard to stop."

"I rejoiced with those who said to me, 'Let us go to the house of the LORD.'"
(Psalm 122:1)

For all its storied history, the World Series rarely captures my attention. There was something different, though, about the series of 2004. The Boston Red Sox had not won a series since 1918, after which they had traded Babe Ruth, the Bambino, to the New York Yankees. Between 1918 and 2003, the Sox had appeared in only four World Series, losing each in game seven.

The curse of the Bambino (as people called it) seemed to strike again in 2004 as the Sox fell to the mighty Yankees in the first three games of the American League playoffs. No team had ever come back after being down three games to none. Boston would need to win four games straight, the last two of them in Yankee Stadium.

The Red Sox won games four and five, and then I turned on my TV. There was a growing confidence in the eyes of the players as they traveled to New York for the sixth game of the series. It appeared that momentum had begun to turn in their direction, and a team that has momentum is on the move and hard to stop.

Boston went on to accomplish what no other team in the history of baseball ever has. They won the championship series against the Yankees after being down three games to none, and then they swept the St. Louis Cardinals in four straight games to win the World Series.

Momentum for Life

Every baseball team goes into the season with the goal of reaching the Series and winning the prize. Some teams break out early, only to fade in the heat of August. Others persist, paying the patient daily dues of disciplined practice on the fundamentals. Likewise, you cannot get where you want to be in your faith, influence, relationships, vocation or physical-emotional health if you are not moving forward.

From priests to presidents, the landscape is littered with the corpses of talented people who failed to maintain the positive momentum of character development. From Bill Clinton's indiscretions to Martha Stewart's deceptions, from the executive failure at Enron to the high-tech meltdown, from the Catholic sex-abuse scandal to a major Protestant denominational leader's admission of an extra-marital affair—people of influence in government, business, and religion alike stumble into the oblivion of moral and ethical failure. And what is true for them is true for all of us. Maintaining life-momentum is imperative if we are going to navigate our way faithfully through a world of clouded moral boundaries.

Pause and take inventory of your life. Are you moving forward (growing, making progress, seeing results) in the following areas?

	Yes	No
Faith	____	____
Influence	____	____
Relationships	____	____
Vocation	____	____
Physical-emotional health	____	____

We are all people of influence. Each of us has an effect on those in our circles of acquaintance, a bigger effect on our circles of friends, and a still bigger one on our family members. Influence is more often about our actions than our words, and it can be negative or positive. Kind words and angry words, conscientious work and slipshod work—each can cause ripples that extend much farther than we can see. That means the integrity we bring to each action is vital, for it sets in motion events we often don't foresee. All progress, all positive influence, all leadership begins with self-leadership.

How would you define self-leadership?

_____

_____

Settling for Lesser Dreams

We dream about the incredible opportunities we have to influence the world for God's purpose. We know that through God's Spirit we can make lasting contributions that benefit the well-being of others. But *having a dream* and having the disciplined, lifelong dedication to *realize that dream* are two different things.

Most good things are the result of a predetermined desire, an ongoing commitment to build momentum for life. Faith is not an instant realization of a desired future, for nothing worthwhile can be acquired at once. *"Now faith is being sure of what we hope for and certain of what we do not see"* (Hebrews 11:1).

Many young people start with dreams of walking closely with God and being used to make a difference on planet Earth. Yet so many bright, rising stars are tempted to compromise their idealistic visions. They begin to work for money instead of meaning. They settle for a job instead of a life calling. They focus their lives on personal achievement rather than enduring contributions. Young people are selling out, and older people are cashing out.

God wants so much more. God wants to build lifelong momentum toward what we were created to become. The apostle Paul compares the life of faith to running a race that requires the impetus of momentum.

> *Do you not know that in a race all the runners run, but only one gets the prize? Run in such a way as to get the prize. Everyone who competes in the games goes into strict training. They do it to get a crown that will not last, but we do it to get a crown that will last*

forever. Therefore I do not run like someone running aimlessly; I do not fight like a boxer beating the air. No, I strike a blow to my body and make it my slave so that after I have preached to others, I myself will not be disqualified for the prize. (1 Corinthians 9:24-27)

Instead of climbing to new heights, too many people plateau when they meet resistance. It doesn't have to be that way. God wants to win the battle for the soul of the world, and it begins for each of us with the management of the world inside. I've learned this the hard way through several conversion-like crises:

• My *marriage*. On June 1, 1992, my wife, Carolyn, and I made the disciplined commitment to start our marriage over. After almost twenty years together we were headed toward divorce. Instead, I had a conversion about investing in that key relationship.

• My *devotion*. On August 17, 1994, I traveled to Korea with a doctor of ministry class from a nearby seminary. As we learned firsthand about the amazing revival sweeping that country, I saw that the real power was in the Korean church's commitment to prayer. I made the disciplined commitment to begin every day with a time of devotional meditation and prayer.

• My *body*. On August 18, 2000, I was at a restaurant and started to feel sick. Seconds later I collapsed and was rushed to the hospital. In the days that followed, a cardiologist said I haven't taken good care of my heart and body. My body fat content was in the 30s—a ridiculously high level—so in October 2000, I started working with a personal trainer. I was converted in the way I eat and exercise.

In the wake of these potentially catastrophic events and my accompanying mini-conversions, I discovered a group of practices that helped me achieve a self-discipline I had not experienced before. These practices cover every key area of my life—spiritual, intellectual, interpersonal, physical, and missional—so that when I follow them faithfully I am a more complete human being. They enable me to build momentum for life.

Model for Living: D-R-I-V-E

I am convinced that every follower of Christ needs to find self-management practices that create momentum for life. Mine are based on the acronym D-R-I-V-E. They are the elements that keep me moving with momentum towards God's promised future, and I believe they can be effective tools for you as well.

Devotion

D stands for devotion. This is the spiritual element. Many persons of faith lack depth and prophetic clarity because their devotional lives are superficial. Daily Bible study and journaling, undertaken with rigorous discipline, vitalizes my devotion to God. I do it first thing in the morning, just like I get ready for the day. If I don't practice this discipline, it takes me only twenty-four hours to lose my fear of God. What we do determines who we become. I want to see life through God's eyes and become passionate about the concerns that matter most to God, and this morning devotion helps me do that.

Put a checkmark beside the words that describe your current devotional life:

___ Nonexistent
___ Sporadic
___ Regular
___ Dry/Boring
___ Invigorating/Growing
___ Meaningful
___ Exciting
___ Stagnant
___ Superficial

My devotional practice is the S.O.N. method that helps me see through the eyes of the SON of God. It involves the Scripture I read for

11

the day, the **O**bservations I journal as I read, and the practical applications I **N**ame for my life. I then take time to express my feelings and thoughts in a written prayer. I'll show you a specific example of what I do when we explore the importance of devotion in Week 2.

Readiness

R represents **r**eadiness for lifelong learning. This is the intellectual element. As a disciple of Jesus (the word *disciple* means learner), I want everything I read and observe to impact the faithfulness and effectiveness of my life ascent. Jesus said, *"My sheep hear my voice"* (John 10:27, KJV); and I want to learn to better recognize his voice.

Many people stop learning once they've received a diploma. They grow redundant and boring. Any of us can grow similarly stale unless we remain committed to expanding our horizons, and that is exactly what this discipline is designed to accomplish. In Week 3 we will look at the importance of nurturing the disciplined practice of lifelong learning, and I'll share with you my personal daily regime.

What are *you* currently reading and/or learning?

Investing

I denotes **i**nvesting in key relationships, beginning with my family. This is the interpersonal element. I'm committed to putting my family before my work and church.

I also invest in other people who are strategic for the mission. All people are equally important to God, but not all are equally strategic when it comes to the expenditure of your time for God's purpose. Maybe for you it's a key group of volunteers who act as unpaid staff or a few certain young people in need of a strong mentor. For me, it's the senior management team at Ginghamsburg Church. They are my "mission critical people," the only people besides my family who can contact me anytime. It's easy to let others set and fill my schedule based solely on who calls and says, "Pastor, I've got to see you today"; but practicing this discipline helps me keep first things—and first people—first. We'll explore this discipline in greater detail in Week 4.

In addition to your immediate family, who is most strategic in your life?

_____

_____

Vision

V indicates a vision for the future. This is the missional element. This is the most critical discipline, the one that all the others point toward and support, because no amount of learning, personal relationships, spiritual discipline, or physical health can give you momentum for life if your life has no purpose. It's critical that you have a vision, because you become your life picture. As the Book of Jeremiah opens, the Lord asks the prophet twice, *"What do you see?"* (Jeremiah 1:11, 13). It's important to see and develop the picture God has given you. You can't live someone else's picture. You have a unique calling; you must become who God has created *you* to be.

Why is it critical to live with vision?

_____

_____

One characteristic of risk-takers and innovators is that they have clear faith-pictures of life. Like Joshua, they need courage to step into their dreams (see Joshua 1:1-9). Like Jeremiah, they must act upon everything God has commanded them; or they will yield to fear. When we begin to relinquish our dreams to fear, we downsize God's vision. We will consider the perils of a lack of visualization later in this lesson. Then in Week 5, we will cover the specifics of visioning for the future.

<u>E</u>ating and <u>E</u>xercise

E stands for eating and exercise. This is the physical element. Sustaining momentum for life requires spiritual, social, and intellectual discipline; but you've got to make sure your body will be around for the future you've envisioned! With the apostle Paul, I want to say, "Do as I do" in all areas of my life (see 1 Corinthians 11:1), including the way I take care of my heart and health.

Since my heart-scare in 2000, I have become much more disciplined about my physical health. I run regularly, work out with weights, and watch my fats, carbs, and sugars. As a result, I have more energy now in my fifties than I had in my thirties. I've come to realize that, as part of my daily D-R-I-V-E regimen, eating and exercising are as spiritual as they are physical. We will address healthy eating and exercise habits in Week 6.

How would you characterize your current eating and exercise habits?
__ **Poor**　__ **Fair**　__ **Good**　__ **Excellent**

This acronym D-R-I-V-E has become my way of life. Romans 12:1 says, *"To offer your bodies as a living sacrifice, holy and pleasing to God—this is true worship."* These are the disciplines that help me grow, with all of them contributing to my whole-life relationship with Jesus Christ. The equation is simple:

Faith + discipline = momentum for life

What's your model for living? Many Christians don't have an action plan for a well-balanced life. If you don't have a self-leadership model that works for you, I challenge you to test and explore this one.

Momentum Busters

To go where God is calling in your life and vocation, you must deal with three momentum busters—attitudes that can prevent you from moving toward the purpose for which God has created you.

1. Rationalization:
"I Make Myself the Exception"

Jerusalem is situated on an uneven rocky plateau at an elevation of some 2,500 feet. In ancient times, every faithful Jew (Israelite) was expected to make the pilgrimage to Jerusalem at least once a year to make an honorable, excellent offering in the Temple—the *only* acceptable place to do so. No matter where you came from, you faced quite a climb to reach the Temple. The journey involved the pilgrim's full commitment of body, mind, and spirit.

Worshipers, while making the ascent to the holy city, sang what are called the Psalms of Ascent (Psalms 120–134). These songs are about reinforcing character, faith, and persistence in the face of resistance.

Just as increasing resistance in exercise fuels momentum and produces results, so resistance in life fuels our momentum, producing desirable results. We learn to strive and thrive through resistance. The resistance equips us with the momentum we need to ascend life's mountains. God gives us the strength to increase our life momentum by allowing resistance to come into our lives.

We learn to strive and thrive through

_____.

We need momentum to move upward. We may be pleased with our physical condition; but unless we work out, we won't stay at our current level, much less gain ground. Followers of Jesus are called to "work out" our salvation knowing "*it is God who works in you to will and to act in order to fulfill his good purpose*" (Philippians 2:12-13). We're in a partnership with God that requires sweat equity on our part!

One of our obstacles to life momentum is rationalization—telling ourselves that we can live at the top without the effort of the climb. "I am the exception," we misguidedly tell ourselves. Because we live in a culture that has a passion for the immediate, we want "easy" and "now";

and we try to make God work that way too. Avoiding perspiration at all costs, we lower the bar. We change God's standard of measure. We turn to sex for sex's sake. We sell out by working for money rather than meaning. By lowering the bar, we arrogantly argue with what we read in the Bible, making ourselves exceptions to God's created moral order. We downplay Jesus' warning that *"the gate is wide and the road is easy that leads to destruction, and there are many who take it"* (Matthew 7:13, NRSV). We rationalize, "That doesn't really mean me."

Trouble is, we're not only to believe Jesus but also to embrace the spirit and lifestyle of Jesus. The road is hard, and rationalizing in one area guarantees that we'll end up rationalizing in every area of life.

Briefly describe a time when rationalizing in one area of your life led to rationalizing in other areas as well: _____

_____

Some people see life's destination as making a lot of money and retiring in the Sunbelt, but that's a downsized goal! The destination of the Christ-follower is not a retirement community of comfort, but a continual journey of ascent where God's purpose comes first.

Some of us have momentum in one area but reach plateaus in others. You may be moving upward in your career while becoming stagnant in your marriage or unfit in your physical body. Remember, all leadership, all positive influence, begins with self-leadership. If you can't lead yourself, you can't really lead anyone else. Until every area of your life experiences the momentum of ongoing care, you won't reach your full potential in influencing other people.

The opening words of the first Psalm of Ascent, sung at the beginning of the journey, are prayers of repentance. As they began their journey, worshipers sang, *"I cry to the LORD . . . 'Deliver me, O LORD, from lying lips, from a deceitful tongue' "* (Psalm 120:1-2, NRSV). In other words, "Deliver me from my rationalization and compromise."

What rationalized, sweat-avoiding habits can you name that you need to deal with?

_____

_____

2. Procrastination: "I Don't Know Where to Start"

Procrastination is another huge momentum buster. In fact, failure comes in direct proportion to procrastination.

Have you ever gone into a test or presentation unprepared? If so, you may have experienced the feelings of inadequacy and self-doubt that procrastination, or the failure to take adequate measures of preparation, feeds. Procrastination attaches itself to your psyche and continues to raise its ugly head through feelings of anxiety and dreams marked by panic, failure, and defeat.

Procrastination is destructive, not only in terms of what we put off today but also in how it attaches itself to the subconscious mind and begins to reproduce itself. *"As he thinketh in his heart, so is he"* (Proverbs 23:7, KJV). Our inner, subconscious thoughts determine who and what we become.

The instructor in Proverbs asks, *"How long will you lie there, O lazybones? When will you rise from your sleep? A little sleep, a little slumber, a little folding of the hands to rest, and poverty will come upon you like a robber, and want, like an armed warrior"* (6:9-11, NRSV).

Procrastination always makes you poor. It leads to poverty not only in your wallet, as the writer of Proverbs warns, but in your spirit as well.

Most of us do well in one area of our lives, though we experience poverty in others. Yet compromise in any one area of life will ultimately become an idolatrous cancer that will consume the rest. Procrastination, failing to do today what shouldn't be put off until tomorrow, sows seeds of lifetime failure.

In which areas of your life do you tend to procrastinate? _____

_____

How are you experiencing "poverty" in these areas? _____

_____

What happens when you don't know how or where to start (or you do know and just don't want to do it!)? We find procrastination showing up in three ways:

1. Defaulting.

We make a commitment to do what's right and to tackle the true priority, but at the last minute we default and do something less urgent or more comfortable.

"But you don't know my schedule," you protest. "I'm not putting things off; life is just too crazy right now for me to cover everything that needs to be done."

Many ancient worshipers never made the pilgrimage to the House of God because they felt overwhelmed by the preparations and hassles. In the winter it snows in Jerusalem, and in the summer it's hot. "It's not such a good day to go up to the House of the Lord," people would say as they procrastinated. In spring or fall, they might cite problems with the traffic, with feeling uncomfortable in crowds, with not having the right clothes, or with not knowing what to do with the kids. "It's easier to stay home," many people would conclude. But nothing worthwhile is easy, and the road to the House of God has always been narrow.

You've got to deal with your big "but"—the big procrastination statements you use on yourself. "But I don't have time to get close to God," or "but I don't have time to exercise because I'm too busy." If you're too busy for D-R-I-V-E, then you're defaulting to lesser tasks.

What's your biggest "but" right now?

_____

2. Feeling Overwhelmed.

Some people feel they have so much to do that they don't know where to start. The pile of ironing has stacked up for four weeks, and you have only two clean shirts left. You don't know where to start, so you go to the refrigerator and dig into some ice cream.

When you're feeling overwhelmed, you must do the first hard thing. In your house, it may mean doing fifteen minutes of ironing before you open the refrigerator again. In your spiritual house, it may mean taking a fifteen-minute walk around your block, putting all your cares onto God before you begin your task list.

Good intentions or professions of belief are not the same thing as commitment. No matter how well intentioned, many folks don't make the commitment to finish the journey. In faith development, altitude requires a journey of exertion. Make the commitment to do the first thing.

Sometimes we need someone to help get us going. For lasting momentum, we need the accountability of a person who is ahead of us, someone who has demonstrated success, accomplishment, and faithfulness in the area in which we are struggling.

This is where the church can play a powerful role. Our church uses a life-coach model, providing classes in everything from fitness to finances. If you commit to do the first hard thing, we'll commit to help you get there. We want your whole life—body, soul, and spirit—to become an honorable, excellent offering to God.

Many people at our church are using what we call a *Transformation Journal*, which is a daily Scripture journal designed to take us deeper in devotion to God. Every Wednesday night, we have a life coach teach on the *Journal* Scriptures for that week, taking people to the next level of growth. We offer classes in a wide variety of areas where people typically get stuck. We know that all of us need coaches who are ahead of us. Just as important, we know that at some point each of us is acting as an example, a coach, even if we're not aware of it.

Many churches offer their own classes and programs designed to achieve similar results in the lives of their members. The study you are participating in now is one such endeavor. Take advantage of this opportunity to serve as coaches for one another, providing both encouragement and accountability.

3. Poor Visualization:
"I Don't Have a Picture of Where I Am Going."

The Bible says, *"where there is no vision, the people perish"* (Proverbs 29:18, KJV). To have vision is to have the ability to see with eyes of faith. Vision knows how to articulate God's promising possibilities for the future.

The Psalms of Ascent are a constant reminder to see, from God's perspective, both the world and our own purpose in it. As the ascent becomes steeper, we need a clear reminder of why we started the climb in the first place.

With the ancient pilgrims, we call on God because we need help: *"I call on the LORD in my distress, and he answers me"* (Psalm 120:1). We want to see life from the perspective of heaven: *"I lift up my eyes to you, to you who sit enthroned in heaven"* (Psalm 123:1). As dangers and temptations lurk around the perilous bend, we need to hang on to the vivid picture of our destination.

As with most spiritual principles, the examples in our own lives can be mundane. They can be as simple as the clutter around us. We let up on discipline just enough to allow cluttered spaces in our lives. They lead quickly to cluttered thinking, which translates to a cluttered spirit and an undisciplined lifestyle. Allow a space to become undisciplined or disorganized, and it begins to take on a life of its own.

The same idea works in other areas of your life. If you allow clutter in your spiritual life, marriage, finances, or anywhere else, it will grow. More clutter will accumulate along the way. Soon you'll have a monster in your life.

At some point, the vision of a clean, well-ordered space disappears. We lose sight of the initial plan. And where there is no vision, there is no road map for change. We get mired in the problem.

**What is one place in your life that is "cluttered"—
that does not fully reflect the excellence of God?**

Our God is a God of order. The metaphor used in Psalm 122:3 is based on the dwelling of God, which is well-designed and strategically built. Jerusalem is *"built like a city that is closely compacted together."* Everything fits: stone upon stone, and row upon row.

Architects begin by designing blueprints—life maps, or visions put to paper. Strategic lives likewise develop from well-designed blueprints. They work out of disciplined plans. You need a life map: a critical plan with a definite starting point.

**What is a healthy step you want or need to take in
the area you have identified?**

The pilgrims who were on ascent visualized standing inside the gates of Jerusalem long before they ever arrived: *"Our feet are standing in your gates, Jerusalem"* (Psalm 122:2). Vision creates momentum that is self-sustaining and self-fulfilling.

Sustaining Momentum

From Genesis to Revelation, we are called to a lifestyle of holiness—*"without which no one will see the Lord"* (Hebrews 12:14, NRSV). "Be holy," the Bible commands at least two dozen times. Holiness actually means wholeness. It means that we are being transformed into God's likeness, that all areas of our lives reflect the One in whose image we were made.

We need a momentum that will carry us all the way up the hill of eternity, where our offering to God is a lifestyle that reflects God's excellence. When our lives are devoted to God's excellent purposes, they are made whole, or complete. God is a God of whole-life excellence in every dimension, yet in our brokenness we rationalize and procrastinate and fail to practice visualization in areas of our lives that are less than excellent.

In one of the early Psalms of Ascent, the worshipers make a commitment to go to God's prescribed place of promise; and they pledge to do so with a positive, proactive attitude: "I rejoiced with those who said to me, *'Let us go to the house of the LORD.' . . . / For the sake of the house of the LORD our God, I will seek your prosperity"* (Psalm 122:1, 9). We must not be content with anything less than seeking God's prosperity, God's excellence, in every area of our lives—and that involves work.

The Bible says we are to work out our salvation and that means a commitment to sweat! The great evangelist Dwight L. Moody said, "We pray like it is all up to God. We work like it is all up to us." Grace is not passive. Grace is active: Our sweat meets Jesus' blood, and that's where the miracle takes place.

The apostle Paul says, *"Straining toward what is ahead, I press on toward the goal to win the prize for which God has called me heavenward in Christ Jesus"* (Philippians 3:13-14, NIV).

Today is the day your sweat needs to meet Jesus' blood. Opportunity is not going to come along and drag you off the couch. You have to put yourself out there. Only you can make the commitment to start the climb.

This study will help you to begin the journey of ascent. Each of the next five lessons introduces one of the life principles of D-R-I-V-E. These five life practices will enable you to build and sustain momentum to make your life an honorable, excellent offering and to reach God's promised destination.

In which area of D-R-I-V-E are you "stuck"?

_____

Name the specific momentum buster that you want to break through. (It may be a favorite rationalization, a habit of procrastination, or an unhealthy picture of your future.)

_____

Complete the following prayer of repentance (based on Psalm 120:2), naming the specific area you want to work on in God's grace and making a commitment to cooperate with God in breaking this barrier:

Deliver me, O Lord, from lying lips and a deceitful tongue. Save me from rationalization, procrastination, and a lack of visualizing your bigger purpose for my life mission. By faith I enter into your salvation from _____ [name of specific sin]. By faith I will work out my salvation by _____ [make commitment to a new discipline outlined in this study]. I welcome and invite the Holy Spirit's work in my life because of what Jesus did on the cross for me. Amen.

Momentum Builders

1. "Conversions" are moments when we experience a major turnaround in our thinking or behavior. If possible, name the time and place of your last conversion: _____

   _____

2. Recall the place in your life you identified as not fully reflecting the excellence of God (p. 21). Visualize how this place in your life would be different if it did reflect the excellence of God. Now describe it: _____

   _____

3. Recall the healthy next step you want or need to take in this area (p. 21). What is the who, what, when, where, and how of this next step? _____

   _____

4. In what ways are you rationalizing (making excuses) or procrastinating (don't know how to start) instead of taking the next step on the journey of ascent? _____

_____

5. A life-map can help us keep a future picture. In the space below, draw (or outline) a map of your own life and where you hear/see God leading you. What is up ahead on your map?

DEVOTION> *Focused commitment of time and energy; dedication; faithfulness; deep affection.*

PASSION> *Intensity; strong emotion; ardor; zeal; motivation.*

"Very early in the morning, while it was still dark, Jesus got up, left the house and went off to a solitary place, where he prayed." (Mark 1:35)

Devotion and passion are powerful motivators, twin emotions that create the energy of momentum in our lives. Many anointed leaders of God have discovered that passion is a greater persuasive force than cognitive belief in determining life direction and behavior.

King David was one such anointed leader. He experienced the hand of God working through his life in powerful ways, becoming the greatest king Israel ever knew. He was called by God for a formidable purpose—to lead a unified nation that honored and served God, one that valued justice, prosperity, and peace. He was known as a man of great faith and confident passion. *"In your strength I can crush an army; with my God I can scale any wall"* (2 Samuel 22:30, NLT).

David was a man after God's heart (see 1 Samuel 13:14; Acts 13:22), fervent about everything he did, from battling Goliath to planning the great Temple. David's passionate heart, however, also succumbed to less honorable endeavors. Following his own pleasures, he became obsessed with another man's wife and then compounded his affair with murder. David's failure was not a result of his cognitive belief but of his unbridled passion.

In a similar way, Satan's attack on Jesus in the wilderness was not directed toward Jesus' beliefs but toward his human passions. *"After fasting forty days and forty nights, [Jesus] was hungry. The tempter came to him and said, 'If you are the Son of God, tell these stones to become bread' "* (Matthew 4:2-3). Satan tempted Jesus to shift the focus of his devotion away from his Father to food and fame. Evil went directly for the jugular vein of Jesus' human passions rather than try to appeal to his cognitive beliefs.

The Smell of Passion

Your devotion reveals what you care about, pointing toward the focus of your deepest desires. People can sense your devotion. They can *smell* your passions. Belief, by contrast, is something you must describe verbally.

My leadership at Ginghamsburg Church has been on an upward ascent for more than a quarter of a century, yet no one knows my political beliefs. I have never shared my political persuasions in a message or allowed partisan issues to be the focus of my ministry.

One weekend I asked my congregation to tell me what I am passionate about. I was expecting them to respond, "Jesus!" but instead they shouted back with one voice, "BASEBALL!" They don't know my political views, but they can smell my passion.

I am indeed a baseball enthusiast, but until that moment I didn't know it was that noticeable. I thought about how they responded. If baseball comes across as a greater passion in my life than God, then I need to realign my heart.

The same principle works at home. Our children pick up on our passion far more than they hear our words. Their views and values are more influenced by the objects of our devotion than by our stated beliefs. Is it any wonder that they readily adopt our zeal for music, money, movies, or athletics while struggling to articulate our beliefs and tuning out our religious traditions after they leave home?

Devotion reflects ultimate values. Devotion reveals true belief. Your greatest enthusiasm betrays your true object of worship. Likewise, motivation can be boiled down to passion. Your passions, more than your beliefs, determine your life actions and directions.

Anyone who struggles with discipline or addictive behaviors understands the power of passion. Have you ever gone to a restaurant determined to pass on dessert, only to be derailed when the server told you about the triple-chocolate cheesecake? Your beliefs tell you that you don't need the high-cholesterol fat calories, but your appetite overrules them. The servers are trained to know that your passions will prove stronger than your beliefs.

Most people think, "If only I could increase my belief in God, things would be different." Most likely it is not your *belief* in God that needs to increase; it is your *passion* for God that must grow in order to give you the momentum to thrive in the face of resistance.

Devotion is stronger than structures of intellectual belief. Devotion reflects what you ultimately care about, what you value. If you're ever in doubt as to what that is, just ask those who know you best what your passions are; and they will tell you immediately. Whatever you value most highly becomes the object of your worship, and what you worship *drives* you! We don't need to increase our belief in God—we need to increase our passion for God!

What do those who know you best say that your passions are? Ask three people and record their responses:_____

_____

_____

Present to God's Presence

I have found that it takes me about twenty-four hours to lose a healthy fear of God. When that happens, my heart turns its attention to counterfeit gods. This is why I must begin each day with the lifelong discipline of devotion.

When I come home from work, I enter the house through the garage, pass through the laundry room, and come into an eat-in kitchen. It has a desk where we put the mail for each other to see, and I find it relaxing to thumb through the day's envelopes when I first come home.

One evening, Carolyn was excited to tell me something, but my first impulse was to check the mail. Carolyn was chatting away about her day, but I was distracted. Partway through the discussion she said, "Wait a minute! I'm talking, and you're not here!"

In the same way, God is always speaking, but we're not always present to the relationship. Does it ever seem to you like God is hiding? The real problem is that we are not aware of God's presence.

Devotion is time focused on God's presence. Because it can be hard work, it requires intentional discipline. My God-stalking efforts involve Bible study, meditation on what I'm reading, prayer, and journaling—using our church's *Transformation Journal* (Abingdon, 2007; see excerpts on pp. 37–38) and the **S.O.N.** method of daily devotion, which we will explore later in this lesson. These practices create in me an awareness of the presence of God, allowing the personal voice of God to speak to me and my life situation each day.

Devotion is time focused on God's presence.

What helps you to focus on God's presence?
QT, Prov. 31, Being outside

A More Passionate Life Focus

The daily practice of devotion, of being fully present to God's presence, continually renews a healthy, passionate life focus. Psalm 121, the second Psalm of Ascent, begins, "*I lift up my eyes to the mountains—where does my help come from?*" The phrase *my help* refers to my meaning, my purpose, and my life-empowerment. Metaphorically speaking, this journey of ascent is to the House of God, the place of God's ultimate purpose and presence in my life.

Many of us read these verses and envision a mountainous setting evoking inspiration and awe. For the Israelite pilgrims who sang this psalm on the way up to Jerusalem's house of worship, however, the mountains held a different meaning. When these psalms were written, the hills contained shrines and altars to pagan gods, counterfeits of the real thing. These subtle sirens tempted travelers to stop short of the ultimate objective and dabble in their destructive influences. Pilgrims could be led

→ Jeremiah 3:23

astray by many brands of over-the-counter gods offering instant remedies for every traveling need. Worried about your financial future? The gods of fertility would guarantee the success of your produce. Love-starved or driven by lust? Sacred prostitutes, male and female, were available to relieve your sexual tension.

Similar influences pervade our culture as well, bombarding us with incessant advertisements for over-the-counter gods, fast-food substitutes, and feel-good potions. There are many gods of immediacy along the road making false claims, offering counterfeit versions of fulfillment, happiness, and meaning. The great temptation for any child of God is to stop short of true transformation and seek mere relief, turning off the road on our way up to the House of God toward the sounds of the lustful sirens. As we ascend the road of God's calling, the voices from the hills grow louder in their attempts to lure us to the cultural shrines that promise immediate relief and self-gratification.

When you *"lift up your eyes to the mountains,"* what "god" offers you immediate relief in times of stress? _Shopping_

Danger Zone

Not long ago I met with two dozen young leaders, challenging them to be everything God created them to be. As I talked, I sat in a comfortable chair with my feet propped on an end table. One pastor had apparently been eyeing my boots as he listened. At the first break of the morning he approached me and said, "Do you just wear those boots or do you really have a bike?" He had recognized my footwear as Harley-Davidson boots.

"I'm getting a bike next month," I answered with a big smile. It would be my first Harley. I'd spent sixteen years saving for it because of our family commitment to live debt-free and not to divert money earmarked for mission. God had used my delayed gratification to build character, but I was eager for my bike's delivery date and had already purchased my riding boots. I was breaking them in that day. This young pastor was the proud owner of a Harley, and he knew the power of the boots and the lure of the bike. For both of us, and many others, the Harley is not just a mode of transportation—it's a passion!

The danger is that our passions tend to take on lives of their own. The hillside shrines call to me as I move into the section of the path marked "mid-life crisis." I shouldn't be surprised when my eyes are distracted by those hillside shrines along the road of ascent. Passions tempt us, saying, "Hey, come over here and I will give you life!" Harley-Davidson has worked hard to create a cult-like subculture with its life-offering promises. The company's slogan is "Live to Ride, Ride to Live"; and I find myself anxious to buy the leathers, ride, and find my life's passion.

Danger zone! *"Do not turn to idols or make metal gods for yourselves,"* Leviticus 19:4 states. *"I am the LORD your God."* Along with many others, I can easily be tempted toward idolatry, showing greater passion for metal than for God. I have been on this journey for a long time, and I need to be conscious of where my relief comes from. That's why the first discipline of each morning involves an intense practice of being fully present to God's presence. I am then reminded, *"Surely the idolatrous commotion on the hills and mountains is a deception; / surely in the LORD our God is the salvation of Israel"* (Jeremiah 3:23). I remember that my help is not found in the promised relief of the hills but that *"my help comes from the LORD, the Maker of heaven and earth"* (Psalm 121:2).

> **What is your "danger zone"? What passion has the potential to "take on a life of its own," tempting you toward idolatry?** pleasing others; feeling guilty @ not enough time w/ God / family.

Wrestling Match

I am drawn to the story of Jacob in Genesis 32. Jacob was going through some kind of peril on life's journey. He was literally in the midst of a process of ascent; and all night long he wrestled with God, who had come to him in physical form. God said to Jacob, *"Let me go!"* and Jacob replied, *"I will not going to let you go unless you bless me"* (verse 26).

Wrestling with God does not mean slipping into church on Sunday and then going back home and automatically enjoying God's blessing. God doesn't respond to the "really quick, here I am" method of devotion. It's all about the relationship. I have been in this relationship with God thirty-plus years, and intimacy in any relationship is hard work. It's an everyday kind of discipline; and I must be willing to hang on to God, to work until resolution and connection emerge. If I let go of God too soon, I am done!

As with Jacob, the residual limp reminds me of my daily dependence. Anyone who has wrestled in school knows that wrestling is a hot, sweaty, uncomfortable discipline. Miracles are not magic. Eugene Peterson says in his book *A Long Obedience in the Same Direction* that anything worthwhile in life comes from a sustained momentum in the same direction.[1] There is nothing quick about leaving a legacy. There's nothing easy about mining the true meaning out of our existence.

Anything worthwhile in life comes from a sustained _____ in the same _____.

Jacob discovered that the God of his ancestors is not to be manipulated for selfish purposes or for instant relief and gratification. Quick remedies offer the illusion of spiritual meaning while denying real truth. Jacob grabbed hold of God and refused to let go. "I will not...I cannot...I must not let go until I live in your (w)holiness!"

God-wrestling is an everyday practice. It is through this daily wrestling that God imparts the compassion and serenity we crave so deeply. Any wrestler or athlete understands the discipline and energy required to be fit for a match. Likewise, every day I need to be disciplined in my devotion to Jesus. I am constantly tempted to use Jesus' name but to trust materialism to provide meaning and security. This is why most of us merely donate to God. When we make a donation, we don't alter our lifestyle; it doesn't cost us anything.

Yet Jesus calls us to sacrifice, to go the way of the cross. He said, *"Whoever wants to be my disciple must deny themselves and take up their cross daily and follow me. For whoever wants to save their life will lose it, but whoever loses their life for me will save it"* (Luke 9:23-24). Heeding Jesus' call that we deny ourselves and take up his cross daily for the sake of the coming kingdom of God is the only way we can find life. Life is not about me right now but about me being a link in the chain of God's generations. It's not about my wants, my passions, or my needs; but it is about my commitment to God's greater purpose and the coming of the kingdom of God!

What is your devotion to Jesus costing you?

_____

The distractions on the hillside tempt me to stop short of Jesus' call to journey the way of the cross. It is hard work to persevere through pain and the rigorous daily discipline of self-denial. The temptation is to stop short of the city of God and to set up camp at the seductive altar of the "have-it-your-way" idols.

Beginning my day in reflection on God's Word continually challenges me to move from the cult of the self to the call of the servant. I can always tell the depth of my devotion by the content of my prayers. When my prayers are "help me accomplish..." or "help me achieve...," then my devotion is weak and shallow. As I come more to the place of "not my will, but yours be done" and "Lord, have mercy on me, a sinner," I am discovering again the deep places of my truest hunger and thirst.

What habits, behaviors, and choices in your life reflect the "cult of the self"?

_____

_____

What habits, behaviors, and choices in your life reflect the "call of the servant"?

_____

_____

Now, take an honest inventory of your prayer life. Put an X on the line below to indicate where the focus of your prayers tends to be (what you spend more time praying about).

My Needs/Desires   **God's Will/Desires**

_____

Sacrifice involves willfully altering my lifestyle to achieve a higher, greater purpose. Every day I must wrestle with God to remind me of the Why and the Who of my life. This practice of devotion, my 6 A.M. wrestling match, renews my life focus, and if I let go of God too soon, I am done.

A More Passionate Life Purpose

The practice of daily devotion renews not only my life focus but also my sense of purpose. The stronger and more compelling the Why, the greater the creativity and energy in my life. A big Why makes for uncompromising integrity. This is why Jesus withdrew, to create a margin of devotion as the first act of his day. *"Very early in the morning, while it was still dark, Jesus got up, left the house and went off to a solitary place, where he prayed"* (Mark 1:35). Devotion was the first discipline of his day. This daily practice renewed the Why in Jesus' life and gave him the resolution to keep his focus on his ultimate God-given date with destiny on the cross in Jerusalem. He did not waver in the face of temptation or abandon the mission amid the frustration of fickle followers.

When I get up in the morning, I shave, shower, and dress before I leave the house. In the same way, I must take the time to cleanse my spirit and dress my life vision before I begin the day's activities. I must take the time to renew God's Why in my life so that I face the day seeking meaning over money, preferring a lasting contribution to the kingdom of God over personal accomplishment and achievement. I will not just settle for a job, because God has given me a life calling. The bigger the Why, the greater my purpose will be.

Devotion brings me back to my true center. My work is not the center of my journey, nor is ministry the center of my life; God is. My identity is that of a servant. Jesus the Messiah didn't assume the head place at the table but the servant position of washing feet. "Staff members" work for money and "volunteers" can drop the task when it is not convenient, but servants sacrifice of themselves for the good of others. If you seek to lead or to affect others by your example, your privileges and rights decrease as your responsibility and influence increase.

Influence is not about personal accomplishment and recognition. It is about serving God by building people. It is not about us. We are servants of God Almighty doing only what God asks of us! When we assume the kneeling posture of servant, we must look up to God. We are reminded that God is not a cosmic waiter at our beck and call, waiting to be motioned over to bless our latest business deal. God is revealed to us through Jesus as servant, and we are most like God when we are serving.

How are you serving God by building people and meeting their needs?

_____

_____

The discipline of daily devotion renews the Why of our lives, giving us a greater sense of purpose and meaning. It reminds us of our mortality and creates a sense of urgency for doing God's work.

Now listen, you who say, "Today or tomorrow we will go to this or that city, spend a year there, carry on business and make money." Why, you do not even know what will happen tomorrow. **What is your life? You are a mist that appears for a little while and then vanishes.** *Instead, you ought to say, "If it is the Lord's will, we will live and do this or that."* (James 4:13-15, emphasis added)

Tragedies and natural disasters at home and abroad remind us that no matter how technologically advanced or wealthy we become, we are not in control. They make us aware of what is really important. We're not guaranteed tomorrow, and we must do the work of Christ who calls us while it is still today. *"As long as it is day, we must do the work of him who sent me. Night is coming, when no one can work"* (John 9:4).

A More Passionate Life Practice

A daily life practice of being fully present to God's presence is the foundation of all other disciplines. God speaks to those who are listening and wants to ensure the success of God's purpose through those same people. The magi who came to Bethlehem to honor the birth of Jesus took the time to discern the voice of God and then went back by another road. Jesus' earthly father, Joseph, was able to elude danger and move his family to Egypt because he was listening to God's directive. The Bible records example after example of people who received vital directives from God that would help sustain personal health, integrity, and strategic focus for the duration of the journey.

God can speak to you today in a way that guides your daily practice. It begins with getting spiritually dressed for the day. Let me show you a specific way I have discovered that connects me to God's presence and purpose each day.

S.O.N. Bible Study Method

Before I open the Bible or my journal, I pray. I ask God to open my heart and mind to new truths, to let me see today's Scripture through God's eyes, and to help me understand it with the heart and spirit of Jesus.

Then I begin with the Scripture. I read it carefully and find myself tuning in particularly to the principles described and demonstrated in the text that will be most helpful to me in ministry to others.

Next, I make Observations about the Scripture, often rereading portions of it and writing down notes about what is happening in the text or story. I also make a note of questions or ideas I have, as well as insights into what God is doing or saying.

Lastly, I Name the practical implications, taking a closer look at the observations and applying them to my own life and context. I look for big principles God wants me to understand as well as simple spiritual truths that challenge me to grow. God often shows me specific steps to take that day in order to align my attitude and actions with God's vision for my life.

Many times I will sum up what I've learned in a prayer of repentance, or ask for wisdom and strength for the day ahead. I take time to pray specifically for people God has put on my heart. God uses this time to give focus to my own personal life and to the strategic direction of the ministry I lead.

What is your current devotional practice?

_____

_____

How might the S.O.N. Bible study method enrich your devotional practice?

_____

_____

Devotion in Motion

God can't steer a parked car. God is looking for people who will take their lives out of park and shift them into drive. John Wesley, the great evangelist who began the Methodist movement, talked about practical holiness and "going on to perfection." You play a part in going on to (w)holiness and creating momentum in your life. So, grab that gearshift, take your life out of park, throw it into drive, and begin moving towards God's place of promise.

F 1 SAMUEL

FRIDAY: THERE MAY BE GIANTS 3/4/05

God's promise of provision does not eliminate obstacles in our walk with him. However, God does provide deliverance as we face those challenges with determination and confidence in God, as David did. The "giants" in our lives will be overcome as we trust in God's power and provision.

Scripture
1 Samuel 17:1-58

Observations

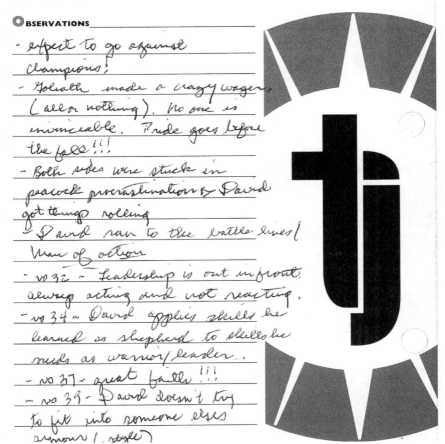

- expect to go against champions!
- Goliath made a crazy wager (all or nothing). No one is invinceable. Pride goes before the fall!!!
- Both sides were stuck in peacock procrastination & David got things rolling
- David ran to the battle lines/ Man of action
- vs 32 - Leadership is out in front, always acting and not reacting.
- vs 34 - David applies skills he learned as shepherd to skills he needs as warrior/leader.
- vs 37 - great faith!!!
- vs 39 - David doesn't try to fit into someone elses armour (style)

transformation journal

A ONE YEAR JOURNEY THROUGH THE BIBLE

NAME PERSONAL APPLICATIONS

"I come against you in the name of the Lord almighty . . . This day the Lord will deliver you into my hands . . . "

~ utter humility - forward action - total faith !!!

- my strength is not in my own ability or resources " it is not by sword or spear that the Lord saves; for the battle is the Lord's . . . "

~ vs 50 " without a sword in his hand (David) struck down the Philistine and killed him "

- David's always "running" to the task of mission,

Prayer · Father, empower me to be today who you need me to me and to be who my Family believes me to be

JOURNAL QUESTIONS

•What characteristics does David demonstrate in this trial? What benefits did David's faith bring to his community?

•What "giants" are you facing right now? What actions can you take that will model David's character as you address these obstacles?

Momentum Builders

1. What would you say you are most enthusiastic or passionate about?

   _____

2. What did the people closest to you say you are most passionate about (p. 27)?

   _____

3. If the answers to the first two questions are different, what does this reveal to you?

   _____

4. If it is true that our greatest enthusiasm betrays our true object of worship, then what is the true object of your worship?

   _____

5. "God is looking for people who will take their lives out of park and shift them into drive." How does this statement apply to you?

   _____

   _____

6. What is one thing God is saying to you about your own devotion? Write your action step here:

   _____

[1] See Eugene Peterson, *A Long Obedience in the Same Direction: Discipleship in an Instant Society* (Intervarsity Press, 1980).

Week 3
Readiness for Lifelong Learning

READINESS> Preparation or availability for service, action, or progress. Prompt willingness. i.e., "Readiness to resume study or continue discussions."

"In vain you rise early and stay up late, / toiling for food to eat—
for he grants sleep to those he loves." (Psalm 127:2)

We spend more time working than doing any other single activity in our brief lifetimes. Most of us will spend more time at work this week than we will spend with our families or friends. And while we may get six to seven hours of sleep tonight, we will have worked eight to ten hours.

God desires for us to make the most of that time and intends for our work to have a purpose. It is not God's will that we toil in vain, anxious labor. Work is meant to be both fruitful and fulfilling. But if we are not intentional about continual growth and improvement, we can spend our entire forty-plus-year careers like the men and women of Israel who walked aimlessly in the wilderness, never to reach their destiny or taste the produce of promise.

Growth and fruitfulness go hand in hand. If I am not practicing a daily, disciplined ascent in my life's work, then I will just keep on preaching the same old sermons, singing the same old songs, and writing the same old books—and my work will not be relevant, fulfilling, or fruitful.

God desires our "work" to be fruitful and fulfilling, but not all of us are experiencing this benefit. Which response best describes your current work/day job?

____ **Just a paycheck**
____ **More frustrating than fulfilling**
____ **Enjoyable, but I don't see how it's fruitful for God**
____ **Fruitful and fulfilling**

An Honorable, Excellent Offering

Remember, our destination is the House of God. In ancient Israel, the temple of God was the only place a Jewish person could go to make an honorable, excellent offering. We no longer make the journey of ascent to the Temple of God to offer bulls, sheep, or doves. Instead, our *life work* becomes the honorable, excellent offering we make to God. Our journey of ascent requires that we have certain daily disciplines, or life practices, in place. Ascent never reaches a comfortable plane or plateau.

To maintain healthy forward momentum for life, I begin my day with a focused time of **D**evotion. Jesus reminds us that the most important commandment calls us to love God with all our *heart* (Matthew 22:37). "Heart" is about who I am at the core of my being. It is the part of me that affects all my thoughts, actions, and decisions. Who I am becoming in Jesus is the most important gift that I have and can offer back to God. It is my acceptable sacrifice.

We must not forget, however, that this commandment also calls us to love God with all our *mind* (Matthew 22:37). Right after I spend time listening to God, I spend time in the discipline or exercise of stretching my mind. This is when I practice **R**eadiness for lifelong learning. It means I'll never get out of school. I study everything from magazine articles and books to websites and newspapers. I read and study about leadership, business, technology, history, and religion. I am interested in church trends, cultural trends, and market trends. More important, I want to know how great leaders of the past stayed both faithful and fruitful.

How can the regular discipline of lifelong learning help your life to be more fruitful?

_____

_____

Jesus told us that we must sustain the never-out-of-school attitude of a child if we are truly to enter into the fruitfulness of kingdom living (see Mark 10:15). Children are constantly learning. For them, everything is adventure. As adults, we can maintain this childlike attitude by the stretching of our minds, which allows our work to continue on the upward ascent of God's purpose. As we commit ourselves to this discipline, this practice of readiness for lifelong learning, our work will be creative, excellent, redemptive, and innovative.

Creative Work

You were created to be creative. This is the work that Jesus wants to release in your life. This is what it means to be created in the image of God.

According to the opening pages of the Bible, God worked for six days and rested for one. God didn't party for six days and then work for one. Work is good or God would not have done it! Work is why we are here on planet Earth. After creating Adam, *The LORD God took the man and put him in the Garden of Eden to work it and take care of it*" (Genesis 2:15). The implications here are powerful: You and I are co-workers; we are co-creators with God.

All work and all creativity begin in your mind. The physical manifestation of any reality begins as a thought. You must conceive something before you can achieve it. This is why the Bible talks to us about renewing our minds (Romans 12:1-2). To renew my mind means I must stretch it.

You must _____ something before you can _____ it.

The first chapter of the Gospel of John tells us that the Logos, or divine intellect of God, became flesh: "*In the beginning was the Word, and the Word was with God, and the Word was God. He was with God in the beginning. Through him all things were made*" (John 1:1-3). We know the Logos as Jesus. "*The Word became flesh and made his dwelling among us*" (John 1:14). The mind of God conceived an idea, and the thoughts became reality.

Like God, we must conceive before we can achieve. When Beethoven wrote the Ninth Symphony, he was totally deaf. Most people think music comes from what our ears hear, but in reality we must think it first. The symphony was first formed in Beethoven's mind. He "heard" it there, and the idea was transformed into physical reality. All physical creation begins as a thought.

Flexible Minds

The Bible repeatedly challenges us to pursue wisdom, and wisdom requires bigger thinking. It requires new thinking. Wisdom requires the exercise of a person's mind. God cannot use narrow-minded people, closed-minded people, or empty-minded people. Jesus said that you can't put new wine into old wineskins (Matthew 9:17), which have lost their ability to stretch.

I hate the discipline of stretching before my physical workouts. I'm tempted to cheat and not do it; but if I don't stretch, I will lose flexibility. God is a God of new things, calling us to sing a new song. God is looking for people who have flexible minds that can receive new ideas, and who will let those ideas be manifested into physical reality. God will not trust the valued, aged wine of redemptive wisdom to minds that are not subject to the practice of stretching—the daily discipline of renewed thinking.

If you are not stretching your mind, God is not going to waste new wine by putting it into an old skin. The obstacle to forward momentum is old thinking. Making strategic plans from old paradigms is a recipe for bursting wineskins. Remember those deadly words: "We never did it that way before." When I am stretching my mind, I am always looking forward to the next new thing.

The obstacle to forward momentum is _____ _____.

My grandfather, with his eighty-something-year-old paradigms, was challenged by the myriad of changes going on in the world. He marveled on one occasion that I could speak on a Sunday morning in Ohio and at

8:00 P.M. that same day in California to an entirely different group of people. It was beyond his comprehension. Years later, up to the time he died, he'd ask, "Did you really do that?"

My grandfather was working from an old mental paradigm, a horse-and-buggy way of thinking. That's how he grew up. He saw his first automobile at age sixteen and bought one at age twenty-two, an incredible paradigm shift for him. Little did my grandfather realize that as he was going about his daily affairs in a horse cart, Orville and Wilbur Wright were stretching their paradigms and developing a new mode of travel that would make possible my same-day, cross-continental schedule. That kind of travel required a shift of thinking.

The same mind-stretching was required with the invention of the cell phone. Until the cell phone, my telephone number was tied to a physical address. You would look up my name in a telephone book, and you would read my address and then my telephone number. Yet when I was speaking in the mountains in the Czech Republic, I could take my cell phone out of my pocket and call my son in Kansas City to ask how his baseball game went. That's a paradigm shift.

Many of God's children let their minds atrophy. God, meanwhile, is looking for people who are willing to exercise their minds so that they may be transformed and renewed. I have the living presence of Christ dwelling within me. Jesus said that we will be able to do the things that he did and to do even greater things (John 14:12). All things are possible with God, but God will not trust this redemptive work to inflexible spirits or minds.

God is looking for people who are willing to _____ their minds so that they may be _____ and _____.

The discipline of daily reading is work. Stretching hurts. Many people tell me, "I don't like to read." Hebrews 12:11 says, *"No discipline seems pleasant at the time, but painful. Later on, however, it produces a harvest of righteousness and peace for those who have been trained by it."* In other words, discipline requires sweat equity; but the benefits of discipline include a bountiful harvest.

What is one area in which you need to stretch your mind?

_____

_____

Excellent Work

The sister of creativity is excellence. God worked six days, and at the end of every day said, "That was good!" At the end of the sixth day, however, God said that *"it was very good"* (Genesis 1:31). God did not stop working when it was good, but only when it was very good. God is a God of excellence.

A commitment to excellence honors God and builds strong self-esteem. When we are able to offer God our best, the result is healthy esteem. Psalm 127:2 says, *"He grants sleep to those he loves."* This implies that fruitful, excellent labor results in restful sleep. When our work reflects the excellence of God, we get to the end of the day and just want to high-five God—"We did good today, God!" We can go to sleep at night knowing that we are getting an incredible return on our investment. This partnership affords us a strong sense of contribution, personal worth, and satisfaction.

A commitment to _____ honors God and builds strong _____-_____.

Excellence is not about comparing ourselves or our work with the work of others. We have a higher standard. The company doesn't set our goal. The union doesn't determine the pace of our work. We work by God's standards.

When I speak at conferences, people ask me which one of my books is my best one. I always reply, "I haven't written my best book yet." I haven't made my best offering to God yet. From a biblical perspective, the best is yet to come. I am on a journey of ascent. The sense of focus comes from my daily discipline of lifelong learning, and the best is yet to come.

God always saves the best for last. Remember Jesus' first water-to-wine miracle? Most party hosts served the best wine first and then brought the inferior product out when everyone was a little tipsy and couldn't tell the difference. Not so with Jesus. *"You have saved the best till now"* (John 2:10). This is what the journey of ascent is about. It just keeps getting better. Even the prospect of death is no threat, for the best is yet to come.

I don't want to get old, but I do want to become aged like good wine. There is a difference. We all have God-dreams for our educations, careers, and marriages, yet many people I know give up on those dreams by the time they're thirty. They begin to grow prematurely old in mind and spirit, losing the ability to stay fresh and flexible in the ascent. By age fifty they want to retire to the beach and stop contributing to God's dream for the world. That kind of retirement is not a biblical option. It is the consequence of people losing their God-inspired momentum.

Moses, a lifelong learner himself, wasn't even ripe for God's picking until he was eighty years old. At the full-bodied age of eighty, he had grown sufficiently in spirit and in wisdom to maximize the fruitfulness of his leadership. Just as Moses was a lifelong learner, you and I must never leave school. We must each practice the daily discipline of lifelong learning. We must hold onto the inquisitive nature of the child within so that we don't miss the incredible wonders of the kingdom of God. Mediocrity does not honor God.

I love Jesus' demonstration of excellence when he healed the blind man of Bethesda (Mark 8:22-25). Jesus spat, rubbed his spit into the man's eyes, and then asked, in essence, "Well, how is it?" The blind man replied, "I can see colors and movement, but everything is kind of blurry. People look like they are trees walking around, but it's okay—really!"

Jesus said, "Hold on. We are not into 'okay' here. Let's give it another go-around." Jesus touched him once more, and the job was complete—

20/20 vision. Jesus didn't quit until the job was done, and done with excellence. Jesus wasn't into mediocrity; to bear the name of Jesus requires that we pursue the excellence of God as well.

What is one way you can pursue the excellence of God in your work/service?

_____

_____

Redemptive Work

What is the purpose of work from God's perspective? Work is an act of worship. *"Therefore, I urge you, brothers and sisters, in view of God's mercy, to offer your bodies as a living sacrifice, holy and pleasing to God—this is true worship"* (Romans 12:1). The Greek word for worship is the same word used for service. Some Bibles translate worship here as work. To worship is to render physical service. Your work is your spiritual service to God. To work is to worship and to worship is to work; it's bringing an honorable, excellent offering to God.

Our culture has reduced the idea of worship to a one-hour weekly event, when worship is really a daily endeavor involving all of our work. The purpose of our work is to render service to God. It is to be a daily part of God's redemptive work in the world.

The Psalms of Ascent remind us of the potential distractions and idolatries that can take us off path and keep us from reaching the ultimate purpose of God for our lives. Psalm 127 calls our attention to one of them: "vain labor" or fruitless work, which is any work you do that is not part of God's redemptive plan in the world.

What makes the difference? It is futile work if you, rather than God, are at the center. It is "in vain" when the motive of work is money. Jesus called this the bigger-barns syndrome. He told the story of a man whose entire motive for working was to make money. After he made a lot of money, he still couldn't see beyond himself as the center of the universe. So he built bigger barns (see Luke 12:18-19). Jesus called that man a fool and later said, *"Do not work for food that spoils, but for food that endures to eternal life, which the Son of Man will give you"* (John 6:27).

Not long ago I spoke with a businessman in his forties working in the field of engineering. "I always wanted to teach at a community college," he remarked. "That is my ultimate goal. When I retire, I'm going to teach at a community college."

I replied, "You mean, if you could do anything in the world right now, you would teach at a community college?"

"Yes," he said.

"Then why are waiting until you retire?" I asked. "Why don't you just go do it now? You have a Master's degree; just go teach in a community college."

You know what he said to me? "I can't afford to."

When our work is driven by the monetary return on our labors, then we are really saying, "My security comes from money, not God's promise of provision." When we do this, we become fearful of the very calling God has placed in our hearts, and we squander the passion God has placed within us. Saying, "I believe in God, but I trust money for my security" is today's version of the bigger-barns syndrome.

Why do so many of us profess our belief in God but trust money for our security? Faith is the ultimate expression of the object of our trust. We've only been given this one life. To waste that life because money is the source of our well-being and provision is vain worship.

Life is too short to work at a job only for the purpose of earning a living. I want a calling, not a job. I want to build a *life*—not a resumé! God has placed a great passion in your heart. Pursue that passion with everything that you profess, and trust God's provision.

If you could do anything in the world right now, what would you do?

_____

What is keeping you from pursuing your dream?

_____

In what specific ways do you need to trust in God's provision?

_____

_____

The measure of work is not the wealth it produces for us but the opportunities it provides for service. Our work becomes an honorable, excellent offering to God as we contribute to the well-being of others. This is true worship!

The Priority of People

We work for the benefit of others. One of the Psalms of Ascent reminds us of the motivation for this life journey: *"For the sake of my friends and of all the people, I will say, 'Peace be within you.' | For the sake of the house of the LORD our God, I will seek your prosperity"* (Psalm 122:8-9).

The gospel is counter to many of the cultural values portrayed in reality programs such as *The Apprentice* and *Survivor*, where the goal is to gain advantage and ultimate victory over your teammates. Work must never exploit people for the purpose of personal profit or selfish gain.

When I am actively participating in the redemptive work of Jesus, my labors will add value, enhance quality of life, and promote connectedness in relationship. When my work is not an act of worship, it will result in the construction of a tower of Babel: *"Then they said to each other, 'Come, let us build ourselves a city, with a tower that reaches to the heavens, so that we may make a name for ourselves' "* (Genesis 11:4). While bigger barns are all about more money, towers of Babel are all about more me. My achievement, my recognition, and my personal success become the driving, motivating forces behind my work, rather than my desire to make a lasting contribution to God's greater redemptive purpose.

What is the real motivating force behind your work? _____

_____

Ross is a Jesus-follower and a passionate car salesperson whose sales record is always near the top at the dealership where he works. Now here's the paradox: several years ago he refused to sell me a car that I would have used credit to buy. Ross was convinced the acquisition would overstretch my finances. He truly seeks the prosperity of others, as the psalmist describes, even at the cost of his own commission.

By their actions toward others, people like Ross demonstrate the power of God. As I emphasized in Week 2, whatever we do or fail to do for people, we do or fail to do for God. We want to be among the ones that Jesus welcomes with great reward: *"Come, you who are blessed by my Father; take your inheritance, the kingdom prepared for you since the creation of the world"* (Matthew 25:34). As we respond to people's true needs—whether hunger, thirst, homelessness, sickness, or even financial imprisonment—we truly serve the God we name.

We're all going to die, and the offering we make to God is all that will live beyond us. Your worship is far more than the songs you sing in church. Worship is the honorable, excellent offering you're making to God through your work as part of God's redemptive purpose in the world.

A Poured-Out Sacrament

When we daily offer our work to God as an act of worship, God makes it a poured-out sacrament in the lives of others. *"Whoever finds their life will lose it, and whoever loses their life for my sake will find it"* (Matthew 10:39). The greater the sacrifice we are willing to make, the broader the scope of influence God will allow us to have in the lives of other people.

The practice of going to work every day provides the opportunity for us to be a poured-out sacrament in the lives of other people. When we place ourselves in God's hands, God is able to use our offering as squeezed-out grapes and broken bread, sustenance in the lives of other people. The key is *staying* in the hand of God on a daily basis, and that's not as easy as it sounds. When we fail to stay available to God by neglecting to practice our daily disciplines, we become more like a marble than a grape, inflexible and devoid of anything to offer others. You just can't squeeze life out of a marble.

> **How would you explain what it means to be a poured-out sacrament in the lives of others?**
>
> _____
>
> _____

The disciplined, daily practice of lifelong learning makes us more useful in God's service to others. Do you know why God chose Moses? Even at eighty years old, Moses was a lifelong learner. Moses was strategic to God's purpose because he was a lifelong student of his culture and time. *"Moses was educated in all the wisdom of the Egyptians and was powerful in speech and action"* (Acts 7:22). We must begin our day by stretching our spirits in reflective study and active listening through God's Word. Like Moses, we must then stretch our minds through the study of the ideas, mores, and preferences of the cultures in which we live and work, positioning ourselves to make the most honorable, excellent offering to God possible.

Innovative Work

It is amazing to note Jesus' methods of innovation as he went about doing the work of God. *"Having said this, he spit on the ground, made some mud with the saliva, and put it on the man's eyes. 'Go,' he told him, 'wash in the Pool of Siloam.' . . . So the man went and washed, and came home seeing"* (John 9:6-7). In her book *Designing Worship*, Kim Miller writes, "God's best work . . . has always been done with amazingly ordinary stuff—water, mud, spit, a piece of stale bread, a barn, a teenage girl, twelve dysfunctional disciples. God uses ordinary objects in regular places with everyday people."[1]

During America's industrial age, Dayton, Ohio, was known as a center of innovation. From its poets (Paul Laurence Dunbar) to its pilots (the

Wright brothers), Dayton looked to the future. Pull-top beverage cans, cellophane tape, the cash register, the movie camera and projector, the parachute, the computing scale, and the electric automobile starter were all invented in Dayton.

An economic report released in early 2005, however, reported Ohio as being next-to-last in the rankings of states that are creating new jobs (Michigan was last). The economies of Ohio and Michigan are dependent on the industries that support Detroit and the automobile industry. The area once known as the industrial belt for its mastery of the industrial age is now referred to as the rust belt because we have not yet figured how to make the transition to the age of information and technology.

When you quit growing, you quit being useful to God. When you quit stretching your spirit and your mind, you plateau. You leave the path of ascent, and your life and work will be neither fulfilling nor fruitful.

People who are committed to the lifelong discipline of learning continue to add value to the endeavors they are committed to. Most folks can readily identify the obstacles and problems inherent in any organization. Take, for example, the twelve spies Moses sent out as advance scouts into the Promised Land (see Numbers 13–14). Ten members of the board readily identified all the "why we can't" barriers, but Joshua and Caleb were able to find the "why we can" solutions and lead the way. They were innovators.

We must be committed to studying innovative practices if we are to become experts in God's future.

Name an endeavor you are committed to:

_____

What is one way you could add value to this endeavor this week?

_____

_____

Practicing Lifelong Learning

Consider three practices of lifelong learning: reading, observing, and doing.

1. Read

First, you should always be reading something. I often ask people who are successful and faithful, who are moving forward on the journey of ascent, what they are reading. I want to know what is feeding and inspiring them. I want to move with people who are moving.

You must always be reading something and must always be ready to share with someone else how it is helping you become better.

Ask three successful, faithful people what they are reading and record their answers:

_____

_____

Which of these books/resources might you be interested in reading?

_____

_____

2. Observe

Second, train yourself to observe. The Bible says wisdom cries aloud from the streets (see Proverbs 1:20). I am observing all the time, seeking opportunities to learn. I am looking for pioneers, people who are ahead of me making honorable, excellent offerings to God. I'm observing older people who are faithfully continuing the ascent ahead of me. I'm watching younger people who are showing signs of budding innovation. I am observing the best leaders and communicators in multiple venues.

When God called me to be a preacher, I didn't study preachers. I studied effective comedians! I figured that anyone who could talk for an hour and have people pay $75 a head to hear him or her had to have something going on. Anytime I have an opportunity to watch a comedian on TV, I study everything the comedian does. It's not that I want to be funny; I simply want to learn about engaging an audience.

The Bible tells us to take the good and separate the bad (see Matthew 10:16; 13:24-30), so I am continually observing the people who are great leaders and communicators. The people in your circle of observation are an important part of your mentoring network.

Who are the people in your circle of observation— the "pioneers" ahead of you?

_____

_____

3. Do

We learn the most from hands-on experience. We retain the most of what we read, see, and hear when we are able to practice by doing.

Writing the first edition of the book this study is based on was a major learning curve for me, as it was the first book I wrote on a computer. All the books I wrote previously were inked out by hand on yellow legal pads. Writing a book with word-processing software was a new experience; but we learn by doing, and I was committed to the challenging—albeit often painful—discipline of relearning how to "write."

"No disciple seems pleasant at the time, but painful. Later on, however, it produces a harvest of righteousness and peace for those who have been trained by it" (Hebrews 12:11). In other words, discipline is painful for a while; but it has one heaven of a payoff!

What can you begin to do today to develop further your own discipline of lifelong learning?

_____

_____

You've got only one life, which will last but a few years on this earth. That life was created to be an honorable, excellent offering to God; and the greatest expression of worship is your work. Commit yourself every day to the practice of learning and keep moving forward on your journey of ascent.

Momentum Builders

1. As a form of worship, our work should always add value to the lives of others. How do you see your work adding value?

   _____

   _____

2. What could you read/study to help you advance God's vision for the world?

   _____

   _____

3. Recall the "pioneers" who are ahead of you (see p. 55). Now specify what you hope to learn from each one:

   _____

   _____

4. What "hands-on" experience would help you to move forward on your journey of ascent?

   _____

   _____

5. What do you hear God saying to you so far as you build momentum for life?

   _____

   _____

[1] Kim Miller, *Designing Worship: Creating and Integrating Powerful God Experiences* (Group, 2004); p. 137.

Week 4
Investing in Key Relationships

RELATIONSHIP> *The state of being related; the mutual exchange between two people or groups who have dealings with one another; kinship.*

"Your wife will be like a fruitful vine within your house; / your children will be like olive shoots around your table. / Yes, this will be the blessing for the man who fears the LORD." (Psalm 128:3-4)

Several years ago I received a call from my sister saying that my eighty-year-old father might need to have emergency heart surgery. Even more difficult were the doctor's words about the low survival rates of the various surgeries being considered for him. I began to think of things I would say at his funeral.

I held my emotions in check as I told myself, "I will do whatever I have to do!"

Later that same day, I went to our church's men's retreat. I had helped plan it and was scheduled to speak. It was Friday evening, and I was in the hotel room when my cell phone rang.

"Where are you?" My wife's voice broke on the other end.

My first thought was that something had happened to Dad. Carolyn began to cry hysterically.

"Toby's dead!" she finally blurted out. Toby was our miniature schnauzer, who was just four months shy of sixteen years old. I had given him to Carolyn for one of her significant birthdays. She had told me that he was the best present I had ever given her. In recent months, Toby had suffered some blindness and various older-dog maladies; but he was still a cherished companion in our empty human nest.

"He's dead, Michael!" Carolyn continued. "I let him out into the backyard for a few minutes, and he didn't come in. I went out into the snow and found him lifeless in the fishpond."

Toby represents many different transitions and memories in my family's collective history. He was around when my grandparents were still alive. He was the family pet of our children's years at home. He was our faithful companion whose image marks the photographs of sacred family passages and memorable Christmases past.

I grabbed my luggage, threw it in my car, and headed for home. There was no time to truly feel my emotions—only the urgency to be who I needed to be for Carolyn and for the care of the dog. "I will do what I have to do...for my wife, for Toby, for the family," I thought. During the thirty-five-minute drive home from the retreat site, my mind was racing. "It's February in Ohio. I need to do something with the dog tonight. How can I dig a burial hole in the near-frozen ground?" I tried to push away visions of Toby paddling helplessly in the water and then drowning—things a good dad should never allow to happen.

My thoughts weren't clear and orderly; they were more like flashes that swirled around my mind. Through the blur, I was aware of my deep sense of responsibility: "I will be who I have to be. I will do what I have to do. I am strong. I am a husband...dad...man...pastor...leader."

My dad's hospitalization less than twenty-four hours ago had left me feeling numb. I was still numb as I drove home.

I'll always remember the picture of what happened next. I walked through the door and saw Carolyn sitting on the couch in the family room. She held Toby, cradled in his blanket, on her lap.

That's when I lost it. I held our dead dog and nuzzled his ear, and I began to cry. It was a long, deep, painful mourning. A tidal wave of emotion engulfed me. I felt an all-encompassing, gut-wrenching pain—the kind of pain I imagine people in my church experience over a child's death, cancer, abusive relationships, or addictions—feelings I typically insulate myself from. I agonized not only over Toby's death, but also over all the senseless deaths that result from tragedy and violence. Grief-stricken, I got in touch with my own human condition of helplessness as I cried, "Why, God? Why?"

Meaning and Relationships

The crisis of sickness and death is the ultimate reminder of life's true meaning, reminding us of what really matters. We are created for relationships. We learn life and faith through the experience of family and friends.

Relationship Rituals

We experience life through a pattern of relationship rituals that is different for each of us. I remember going to my grandparents' house for lunch every Sunday. My uncle's family was usually there too. I can still picture the seating arrangement in that crowded back-porch-turned-year-round dining room of my grandparents' home. My grandfather was always at one end of the table and my dad at the other. I sat next to Granddaddy and across from Uncle Thomas. Beginning in 1996, when my grandfather died, holiday meals found me in his former seat, with my father still at his post on the other end of the table.

Listening to the tribal stories around that table, I learned my identity. Through our relationship rituals, we transmitted values from one generation to another. It was there that I heard stories of our family's faith, and there that my grandmother taught me my first Bible verse, John 3:16. As a very young child I was sitting at that table when I first met a person of another race—a Japanese seminary student. Our family played board games and, with equal intensity, debated political ideology around that table.

I experienced good and bad, function and dysfunction. Most of all, I learned that God loved the world of people—all the people that I had experienced and talked about at that table. Through the relationships around that table, God's love took human form. The family table is where I discovered the sacrament of life.

While holiday meals can make me sleepy, with each passing year I'm less tempted to nap when my family is making precious holiday memories. I force myself to stay awake and look around, remembering that nothing will last forever. I want to breathe in the awe and wonder of witnessing my children interacting with their grandparents. I don't want to miss the experience of these relationships while I'm living in the middle of them.

Describe the dinner table ritual in the home where you were raised.

_____

_____

We miss out on life and meaning if we are not making relationships a priority on any given day. People are created for relationships, and it's in the context of our relationship rituals that we find meaning.

What are the relationship rituals in your family/extended family in which you find meaning?

_____

_____

_____

The Value of Life

I can't control life. I can't even control what happens in my own backyard! I want to think that I can always make my family safe, but look what happened to my beloved pet. I am still dealing with feelings of guilt over my own responsibility: Why did I install that fishpond? Why didn't I put a fence around it?

I'm facing the age-old quandary of Job: Why do bad things happen to good people? The day after my meltdown, I read about Moses' death and the grief of the Hebrew community; and I wrote in my journal, "Maybe death is what makes life so valuable!"

Life repeatedly informs us that we are not in control. Devastating events remind us that no matter how wealthy or advanced our society is, we cannot control the aging of a human life, the actions of other people, or the groaning of the earth. Our wealth and technology ultimately cannot protect or save us.

What was the last crisis that caused you to realize you are not in control?

_____

What did this event teach you?

_____

_____

Did you take any positive steps toward the people in your life at that time; and if so, what were they?_____

_____

People Matter

Life is not about the stuff we own or accumulate. It is not even about personal accomplishment. Life is about people. We can replace stuff, but we can't replace people!

Carolyn repeatedly asked herself the question, "Would I have done anything different in the weeks before Toby died?" Her answer was, "I would have held him more."

Carolyn takes her life's work very seriously, and thus she was working on the computer in an upstairs bedroom of our home that fateful night. She sent a last email at 9:27 P.M. and went downstairs to let Toby out. Her plan was to hold him in his blanket and warm him up when he came inside—but he never came back.

Her thought about spending more time to hold Toby led Carolyn to other thoughts as she reflected later in the week. "Here's the question it makes me ask," she said, "Am I spending enough time with my mother?" Carolyn had not seen her eighty-five-year-old mother in two months. Toby's death had served as a sobering reminder of life's true meaning.

Are you spending enough time with the important people in your life? Who might need more of your time and attention? _____

_____

Margins

In Psalm 128 (another Psalm of Ascent), notice the integration of work and relationships as an expression of worship. Like D-R-I-V-E, the psalm begins with **D**evotion to God. *"Blessed are all who fear the LORD, who walk in obedience to him"* (verse 1). Every day, devotion is our act of getting in touch with God. What happens as a result? *"You will eat the fruit of your labor; blessings and prosperity will be yours"* (verse 2). When we fear the Lord, our work becomes an honorable, excellent offering to God.

The psalm then moves from work to relationships. The two don't compete against each other; they complement each other. *"Your wife will be like a fruitful vine within your house; / your children will be like olive shoots around your table. / Yes, this will be the blessing for the man who fears the LORD"* (verses 3-4).

When the object of our devotion is right, our work and relationships unite as an honorable, excellent offering to God.

Think of the amount of time and energy we spend at work and with our loved ones each week, compared to the paltry hour we spend at church. God is not nearly as interested in the little religious ceremonies we call worship services as in how we live our lives day to day. Our work and our relationships are not separate from our relationship with God; they are the primary expressions of this relationship. They are the truest demonstrations of our worship.

Our Work + Our Relationships = Worship

If we want to honor God—to bring an honorable, excellent offering—we must create and maintain margins for the key relationships in our lives. On a piece of paper, the margin is the empty space. Margins in life are the blank spaces on our calendars—our sacred spaces. You dare not allow your margin for relationships to fill up. When we keep open spaces and time for relationships, we honor God.

Isaiah 5:8 says, *"Ah, you who join house to house, who add field to field, until there is room for no one but you, and you are left to live alone in the midst of the land!"* (NRSV). In other words, all you do is work. You are consumed in expanding your property (joining house to house). You burn the candle at both ends to ensure a good harvest for your fields.

We are created for relationships, and relationships are developed in the margins of our lives. Acts of kindness are done in the margins. When we don't have any margins, people leave us alone because we are always on the edge.

Relationships are developed in the _____ of our lives.

Trouble in the Margins

We get into trouble when we allow our work to fill the margins that are meant for our relationships. That's what happened to Carolyn and me. We allowed ministry to become a priority over our relationship, so that after twenty years of marriage we looked at each other and didn't know one another—let alone like each other! The problem was that we had allowed zero daily margins for our relationship.

This is a mistake of youth. Many people fall into it, as did Carolyn and I. Unfortunately, too many of us fail to figure out the problem until we are forty or fifty. Some never get it. In our youth, we discover that it is easier to focus on a task that can't scream at us and say, "You aren't meeting my needs!" Tasks reward us without talking back. Without realizing it, we learn to focus on tasks rather than relationships.

In marriages, it begins around the time you are supposedly making a commitment of lifelong time and energy to your partner. When you are dating, you are focused on building a relationship. You are finding out what pleases the other person. You explore what the other person likes and dislikes, and you listen to each other's deepest needs. Then you become engaged. At that point you no longer focus on the relationship; you center on planning the wedding, a task that begins to swallow up valuable energy formerly invested in the relationship.

When Carolyn and I became engaged, we were no longer listening to each other's thoughts and sharing our dreams. Rather, we were doing chores and making arrangements. Then we got married and said, "Okay, as soon as we get out of school, we'll have time for each other and we'll work more on our relationship." We didn't.

By now a pattern has developed—a practice of postponement that you too may have experienced. "After grad school we're sure to get more time together," you say to one another; then, "When we get away on vacation this summer, we'll have two weeks just for us." The vacation flies by and soon you're rationalizing again: "When you get settled in your new job, then we'll work on the relationship."

It's not long before children come into the picture, and soon this habit of relational postponement is the only way you know to function. From toddler tears to the high school years, there are no real breaks in the parenting schedule, no weeks when the kids turn to you and say, "We'll take care of ourselves this week; why don't you two work on your relationship?" Finally, when the kids leave and the nest is empty, you wake up one morning and look at each other and say, "Who the heck are you?"

Living Fully Today

In 1938, Thornton Wilder wrote a Pulitzer Prize-winning play called *Our Town.* It tells the story of a young woman named Emily who dies and is given permission to return to the earth for one memorable day. She can pick any day from her lifetime and relive it moment by moment.

Emily chooses to go back on her twelfth birthday because she remembered it as a happy day. She is soon frustrated, however, at the indifference of those she loves. She wishes to engage in life with them but painfully observes that they are just going through the motions, taking each moment totally for granted. As she stands by and watches her birthday take place, she tries to stop it because she can't take it anymore!

She is reliving her special day, and yet no one is experiencing the significant moments. People aren't even looking at each other. Emily cries out, "I can't. I can't go on. It goes so fast. We don't have time to look at one another. . . . Do any human beings ever realize life while they live it?—every, every minute?"[1]

Jesus cautioned about this human tendency. *"Therefore do not worry about tomorrow, for tomorrow will worry about itself. Each day has enough trouble of its own"* (Matthew 6:34). Similarly, James 4:14 states: *"What is your life? You are a mist that appears for a little while and then vanishes."* The prophetic implication: live fully today.

Each of us is responsible for our own schedule, for how we will order today. If we don't prioritize how and with whom we spend our time, circumstances and other people will decide for us.

Who or what most often determines your schedule and priorities day by day?

_____ **I do**
_____ **Circumstances**
_____ **Other people**

Our intentional schedules become our offerings to God. We must prioritize how we will spend our days, how we will create and maintain margins for relationships. Relationships provide us with ultimate meaning, but we must create the margins wherein they will flourish.

How would you describe the margins in your life?

_____ **What margins? I don't have any margins in my life right now.**
_____ **My margins are a little cramped; I need to allow more time for relationships.**
_____ **My margins are just right. I have enough time for the relationships in my life.**

What relational disciplines do you need to observe in order to make an honorable, excellent offering to God? _____

_____

Mentoring

God's strategy for the transmission of faith and biblical values to future generations involves mentoring-based relationships. It's God's plan for passing the DNA of the kingdom of God from person to person, generation to generation.

The transmission is fragile, however, and the handoff has great potential for a fumble. Judges 2:10-11 reminds us: *"After that whole generation had been gathered to their ancestors, another generation grew up who knew neither the LORD nor what he had done for Israel. Then the Israelites did evil in the eyes of the LORD and served the Baals."* The people faithfully served God during Joshua's lifetime, but the next generation did not maintain the values of their parents.

There is a critical difference between ideals and values. Ideals are what you want; values are what you truly live. Your ideals might be that you raise your children to be faithful followers of Jesus, go to college, have fruitful and fulfilling careers, and marry persons of faith, integrity, and intelligence. Values, however, are the real-life priorities that determine your (and their) actual choices. Values are demonstrated through our behaviors more than our cognitive beliefs. The challenge is that our values and our beliefs don't always line up: *"For I have the desire to do what is good, but I cannot carry it out. For I do not do the good I want to do, but the evil I do not want to do-this I keep on doing"* (Romans 7:18-19). How you invest your time, energy, and money are the true indicators of your values.

Many people in the church have biblical ideals but live secular values. They are functional atheists. In the end, our children (or those we have influenced) will inherit and live out our values, not our ideals.

What values do you want to pass on?

_____

_____

_____

_____

How are you currently spending your time, energy, and money?

_____

_____

_____

What does this reveal about your true values?

_____

_____

The People in Your Heart

Our first mentoring responsibility is to the people we have in our hearts—our children or those who are emotionally close to home. Psalm 128 reminds us of the priority of the home and the values transmitted therein: *"Your wife will be like a fruitful vine within your house; / your children will be like olive shoots around your table"* (verse 3).

The women and men who fear the Lord make the mentoring of their families in the values of the Kingdom a major priority. This means our families become a higher priority than our work. When we keep God's practical life disciplines on a daily basis, we make time priorities for our spouses and children, knowing that those closest to us will be adopting our values.

When Jonathan was in college, Carolyn and I moved to Philadelphia for five weeks to experience his last baseball season at the University of Pennsylvania. From a career perspective this might not have been perceived as a wise decision. But my first "profession" is transmitting my kingdom of God values to the next generation.

Our children follow our values, and our truest values are demonstrated through our time priorities. Parenting is a lifelong intentional time schedule, a career of mentorship. We made a huge investment of our time in Jonathan that spring, and it was a blast. We made memories so precious that Carolyn and I wouldn't trade them for anything. An amazing side effect of this whole scenario was that the church continued to grow without me. People need to see leaders who demonstrate the priorities of the kingdom of God in their primary relationships.

The opposite effect could have occurred. What a burden we would have put upon Jonathan if he had been out there trying to prove himself to us, to get our attention, or to free himself from negative self-talk we had instilled into his life.

Whether we're twenty-five or sixty-five, we can choose daily to invest in our key relationships—the people in our hearts.

> **How are you choosing to invest in your key relationships—the people in your heart?**
>
> _____
>
> _____

The People in Your Scope

The second mentoring responsibility we have is with the people in our scope—those strategic to God's mission in our network of influence. All people are equally important to God, but all people are not equally strategic to the investment of our time for God's mission. Jesus ministered to the multitudes, but he strategically spent the majority of his time mentoring his twelve disciples. The ultimate test of success is not what we accomplish or achieve but whom we develop.

All of us must be strategic when it comes to the time we spend with people. As a pastor I learned early on to mark my calendar with strategic think time and strategic people time. It may take two or three weeks for some people to get an appointment to meet with me. I must be a good steward of the time that God has given me, and I must name my own priorities.

You make an impact in the world by making a difference in the lives of other people. It is too easy to become distracted by the wrong priorities. Pastors begin to focus on building programs. Businesspeople pour their energy into building companies. Teachers turn their attention to building lesson plans.

Whatever your type of work, the priority is building people. The ancient Jewish worshipers sang this value as they linked the measure of their work to its influence on people: *"May you see the prosperity of Jerusalem . . . [and] / may you live to see your children's children"* (Psalm 128:5-6). The call of Jesus is a call to make time outside our homes and jobs for a greater purpose in the world—investing in God's mission through the lives of people.

Whatever your type of work, the priority is

_____   _____.

When I look at where I am and what I've accomplished in life, I envision a circle of people who are standing around me. They are the teachers, coaches, youth mentors, professors, businesspeople, and others who supported Carolyn and me when we made the choice to go into ministry. They are all surrounding us with words of encouragement, reminding us to be faithful in finishing the race well.

Who is in that invisible line of people standing behind you? (Teachers, coaches, scout leaders, church leaders, campus ministers, professors, businesspeople, others?) Who has encouraged you, given you a break, or even supported you financially? Whose investment in your life allows you to stand where you are standing today?

_____

_____

_____

Now it's my turn to stand behind others—the people in my scope. One of the persons in my scope whom I regularly set aside time to meet with is Mike Berry, pastor of a church twenty miles east of Ginghamsburg Church. Our bishop was planning to close this aging, dying church; and he asked us if we'd take it under our wing and take one last shot at redeveloping it.

God raised up Mike, who had been part of our church. As a civil engineer, Mike had no formal seminary education; but he sensed God's call to invest himself as pastor of this church. What's happening there has been nothing short of resurrection—a resurrection that mimics Mike's own conversion.

Fourteen years ago Mike stopped drinking, but a lot of things in his life didn't improve. "I was a recovering alcoholic, and I was taking out my unhappiness on anyone who got in my way," he says. His wife, Tracy, had moved out and taken their two children with her. In one last-ditch attempt, they decided to try church before resorting to divorce. "We came to church and something happened about ten minutes into the sermon," says Mike. "The Holy Spirit got hold of us, and things never been the same."

Mike and Tracy rebuilt their marriage around God. "We have grown together, we have grown in ministry, and we have been blessed because of this great God we found," Mike says.

It was a seven-year journey between Mike's conversion and what he is doing today as a pastor. Mike has learned most of what he knows by being mentored through Ginghamsburg's example. "They asked me to take food to a needy family," he explains. "Then they asked me to pray with the family when I got there. They asked me to lead a Christian twelve-step group, and then to become a care pastor. A couple of years later, they asked me to conduct a funeral. Each time, I said 'I can't,' but with each new experience I learned to tap into God's strength."

Mike meets regularly with me for a "Tuesday at two" mentoring session. He asks me to share experiences and ideas for reaching more people for Jesus Christ. "I usually come with a list of questions about my own walk with the Lord or about how to lead a church more effectively," Mike says.

When Mike became pastor of the church, attendance was seventy to eighty persons a week. Within eighteen months, it was climbing past 150. "The momentum of the church has changed from relatively flat and dead to enthusiastically mission-driven," says Mike. "Now ministry is happening every day of the week, from our food pantry to small groups meeting in homes. And I'm still putting family above ministry in my own priorities. My wife and family are located immediately after my personal relationship with Jesus."

"My greatest fulfillment," Mike says, "is that God could use a bottom-feeder like me, someone so off-track in life, to help others become new creatures in Christ, to grow and change."

I am thankful to be investing in this key relationship.

> **Who are you standing behind? Who are you parenting, mentoring, coaching, encouraging, managing, or leading? Who is receiving the intentional, strategic time in your schedule for relationship building?**
>
> _____
>
> _____

Remember, the investment you are making in people today is the only one that will live beyond your lifetime; so invest wisely, reminding others to be faithful and finish well.

Momentum Builders

1. Review the relationship rituals in your family/extended family (p. 60). What makes each of these rituals meaningful?

   _____

   _____

2. Recall the important person in your life you identified who needs more of your time and attention (p. 61). Brainstorm a list of ways that you can invest in this key relationship:

   _____

   _____

3. Think about the idea that **Our Work + Our Relationships = Worship**. Do you lean more toward work or relationships?

   _____

   What can you do to balance the equation in order to make an excellent, honorable offering?

   _____

4. Select one of the persons outside your immediate family whose life you are influencing toward God (p. 69):

   _____

   How has God used you in the past to help "build" this individual- contribute to his or her growth?

   _____

   _____

   What kind of future investment do you sense God calling you to make in this person's life?

   _____

   _____

5. What is one action step that God is pressing on your heart—something you need to say to someone, schedule into your day, or do as a relational investment?

   _____

   _____

---

[1]Thornton Wilder, *Our Town* (HarperPerennial, 1938, 1998); p. 108.

Week 5
Visioning for the Future

VISION> The act of seeing or the ability to see; a picture formed in the mind; imaginative foresight; a supernatural apparition.

"Our feet are standing in your gates, Jerusalem." (Psalm 122:2)

We live in a time of exponential and revolutionary change. If our life's work is to be an honorable, excellent offering to God, we can't ever afford to become content or comfortable staying where we are.

The Power of Vision

The essence of faith is vision. *"Faith is being sure of what we hope for and certain of what we do not see. This is what the ancients were commended for"* (Hebrews 11:1-2). These verses from Hebrews 11, a chapter that defines the hallmarks of faith, showcase people of God who are always stretching forward. They long for a better world, a heavenly one, where the peace of God rules for every person. As long as one person lacks the peace and wellness of God, the love and purpose of God compels the true follower of Jesus forward for the well-being of the planet.

Abraham could not be content with his personal wealth or the rich blessings of family that he experienced. At a ripe old age he left every-thing that was familiar to make a journey of ascent. *"For he was looking forward to the city with foundations, whose architect and builder is God"* (Hebrews 11:10). Faith is looking forward, living with a forward focus. Abraham's task and ours is to work together with God for a better world.

Until I came into a relationship with Jesus, life was all about me. When Jesus came into my life, I became a partner with him in re-imagining God's purpose for planet Earth. We're working together, building a heavenly planet, a place where the peace of God rules for every person. If one person in the world does not have God's peace, then my call is to start another worship celebration, preach another sermon, build another relationship, or strike up another conversation.

Life isn't meant to get easier with increased age and income. My job is to be on a life-long journey of ascent. With the power of vision, I am always moving forward to become my best in the world and for the world.

Vision is the natural result of living in the fullness of the Holy Spirit. On the day of Pentecost, the Apostle Peter quoted from the prophet Joel: *"In the last days, God says, I will pour out my Spirit on all people. Your sons and daughters will prophesy, your young men will see visions, your old men will dream dreams"* (Acts 2:17). Through the Holy Spirit we have access to the mind of Christ.

This is why I make it a daily practice to intentionally envision God's purpose and direction for my future. Establishing a daily discipline of envisioning God's future is critical. It allows me to: 1) formulate a life picture; 2) articulate a healthy, positive life attitude; and 3) initiate strategic life actions.

> **Why is envisioning God's purpose and direction for your future so important? What does it enable you to do?**
>
> _____
> _____
> _____

1) Formulate a Life Picture

All physical realities begin with a mental picture. Vision is about formulating, developing, and giving birth to that new reality. God's vision is developed and birthed through real followers of Jesus. Just as God birthed Earth's Savior through the available womb of a servant named Mary, God is still seeking available servants through whom miracles for the salvation of the world can be born. Every new creation begins in the mind of God. *"In the beginning was the Word, and the Word was with God, and the Word was God.... The Word became flesh and made his dwelling among us*" (John 1:1,14, NIV). This pattern starts with Creation itself. God conceived and articulated the thought, and the Word became material reality.

The architects who designed your office, church, or home didn't start with a bulldozer. Before a shovel ever touched the ground, they saw something in their minds—pictures in detail. They articulated them through blueprints used for the actual construction. Every single piece in those buildings began with a picture in a person's mind.

The vision process works the same for you and me. You must be able to conceive an idea before you can achieve it! God wants to birth a miracle through your life's work, but you must be willing to *receive* it by submission to Jesus' authority in your life. You then have to *conceive* the big idea of God through the disciplines of daily **D**evotion and **R**eadiness for lifelong learning. As you gain skill in the practice of active listening— "*Be still, and know that I am God*" (Psalm 46:10)—God will *achieve* miracles through you.

The sequence is powerful: receive, conceive, and achieve. It results in visioning—the disciplined practice of formulating God's specific purpose for your life.

What are the three sequences in the vision process?

_____   _____   _____

What is the result of this process?

_____

_____

Jeremiah was an effective prophet, but before he could be used by God, he had to formulate God's vision. The first question God asked Jeremiah was, "*What do you see?*" (Jeremiah 1:11, 13). All physical realities begin with a mental picture. This is why you have to be careful about the pictures you nurture, and why everything you allow into your mind truly matters. Your thoughts become the root of your physical fruit.

People tend to live with either a microscopic view or a telescopic view. If you have a microscopic view, your perception of life is based on your current circumstances: what you see, what you feel, and what you hear in the present moment. If you have a telescopic view, you are always looking forward to what God is creating in the future.

Which view do you tend to have?
_____ **microscopic**   _____ **telescopic**

A person with a microscopic view tends to focus on life's problems, on obstacles and limitations. Microscopic people often approach life with a scarcity mentality. Some of Jesus' disciples did that. When he presented them with the challenge of feeding 5,000 people, all they could see were problems, obstacles, and limitations. "Where are we going to get the money?" "There are too many people." "The closest food is more than an hour away." (See John 6:5-7.)

While microscopic people focus on problems, telescopic people see the possibilities. They have confidence that *"all things are possible with God"* (Mark 10:27).

The prophet Elisha had a possibility focus. He had become a thorn in the side of the king of Aram, who was seeking to destroy Israel. The king of Aram sent out spies to discover Elisha's whereabouts. They learned that he was in a city called Dothan, or perhaps on its outskirts; so the king dispatched an impressive fighting force of horses and chariots. They came by night and surrounded the city.

Upon awakening in the morning, Elisha's servant discovered the imminent danger. He had a microscopic response and was ready to run up the white flag immediately. He asked in panic, *"Oh no, my lord! What shall we do?"* (2 Kings 6:15).

Elisha, on the other hand, was not looking with the eyes of his head. He was seeing through the eyes of his heart, looking forward to what God was creating in the future. *"Don't be afraid. Those who are with us are more than those who are with them"* (verse 16). What on earth was Elisha talking about? There was a sum total of two: Elisha and his servant. "*And*

Elisha prayed, 'Open his eyes, LORD, *so that he may see.' Then the* LORD *opened the servant's eyes, and he looked and saw the hills full of horses and chariots of fire all around Elisha"* (verse 17).

The servant saw the urgency of the immediate crisis, and Elisha saw the armies of heaven.

I am a telescopic person. I take time every day to envision a better reality. I can't conceive of retirement because I am constantly renewing my sense of mission by formulating a picture of what God is creating in the future. In fact, my picture is so big that sometimes I worry, "I am fifty-five; how am I going to get this done by the time I die?"

Vision can be defined as a promising picture of God's preferred future. It creates greater energy and generates bigger strategic actions. It gives energy to initiate and sustain the journey of ascent.

What happens when we focus on the promising picture of God's preferred future?

_____

_____

Think of a specific time when vision gave you the energy to work toward God's future:

_____

_____

Vision Focuses on a Destination

Vision is focused on the promised destination. Carolyn and I would be heading to Florida on spring break. We couldn't reach the Ohio state line before our kids would say, "When are we going to get there?" and "Are we there yet?" Most parents have heard that question a zillion times.

One of the early Psalms of Ascent, sung toward the beginning of the journey to Mt. Zion, contained a visual reminder of the destination. The people's intention was to *"go to the house of the* LORD*"* (Psalm 122:1). What was the picture these Israelite worshipers held in their heads? *"Our feet are standing in your gates, Jerusalem"* (verse 2). They held onto that picture, a vision of their destination, until they got there. That is similar to the formation of our own blueprint for the realization of God's future in our lives. Visioning is a daily process of formulating and refining our own life calling.

I have been following the plight of Sudan for years, where a lack of food, the spread of disease, and the ongoing conflict has torn apart the lives of more than three million people, mostly children and women. One morning several years ago, after my time of **D**evotion, I spent some time reading about the Sudan crisis. (**R**eadiness for lifelong learning demands that I read a lot and stay informed about the world.) God began to give me a picture of what we could do.

Citing Isaiah 58, I reminded the congregation, "You have power with God by your actions toward people, especially people in need." One Sunday I held up a newspaper photo of Sudan, which was next to a photo ad in the same section of the paper for a new BMW. Then I said, "It says 770,000 people are on the verge of death because of starvation, and I didn't even know about it. I'm very aware of the BMW sedans, including the twelve-speaker sound system and the sixteen-position reclining seats. What bothers me is that I'm far less aware of the Sudan." Why are we well-informed about the *sedan* but oblivious to starvation in the *Sudan?*

We began to wake up from our selfishness, giving generously and sacrificially. Our middle-school students alone raised $4,000 to build two fresh-water wells. A congregation-wide offering sent $312,000 to our denominational relief agency, funding an agricultural-development program assisting more than 5,000 Sudanese families.

A few months later, the vision began spreading to others, including a cell group of servants in the church who conceived, articulated, and achieved an additional offering for hunger relief. The idea was for each person in our church to fast one meal a week and put the cost of that meal into an envelope. These would be collected as a special Easter offering and given toward Sudanese hunger relief. They called it Fast for Famine.

By the following Christmas, our "Miracle Offering" raised $530,000. The next year our Christmas Miracle Offering topped one million dollars! The money took us into the second year of our five-year child protection and development program and allowed us to launch a four-year project to provide safe water and sanitation for nearly a quarter of a million people.

That's why I keep praying, reading, and learning about the Sudan. One morning a few years ago I sat at the breakfast table and drew a picture for Carolyn of the orphanage that I envision our church constructing for the children in the Sudan. I saw the picture complete with a guesthouse so that we can have medical and support teams on the premises twelve months out of the year. Elsewhere there would be dormitories, classrooms, and a chapel. We will then raise scholarships for each of the children who live in the orphanage to attend Africa University.

My sketch was not a sudden, hastily assembled plan. It represents a vision that grows and is refined every day, a blueprint for the realization of God's picture. I take time every day to visualize God's promised future. I know that if my vision is fuzzy or clouded, this will affect everyone I influence and am connected to. How great the cost would be if I allowed God's vision to be interrupted and ultimately omitted from the lives of those in my circle of care. We must faithfully receive, conceive, and work to achieve the picture of God's promised destination.

As we work toward God's promised destination, it pulls us upward to bolder life actions. When you and I are dreaming God-size dreams, we don't have the time to contemplate retirement. People retire because they get tired of doing the same old things, but God creates new wine that makes our life's work and creations new every morning!

What happens when we focus on and work toward God's promised destination?

Vision Inspires Perseverance

Vision also inspires perseverance. After Moses' death, Joshua accepted the call and challenge to lead God's people into the land of promise. *"I will give you every place where you set your foot, as I promised*

Moses" (Joshua 1:3). After making this promise to Joshua, God then provided a more detailed blueprint for a vast expanse of territory that extends from the Euphrates River in the east to the Mediterranean Sea in the west (see verse 4).

God's promise was a done deal. All Joshua and the people of God had to do was keep on stepping forward. In the verses that follow, God exhorted Joshua not to stop, look back, or deviate to the left or the right but to persevere in the face of opposition and conflict. God told him, in effect, "Don't settle for anything less than the realization of the place of promised destination that you visualized when you first heard Me call your name."

Like Joshua, I just keep walking toward the vision God gave me when I came to a little country church in April 1979. I was very concerned with discovering God's mission for the church. So I established, as my first priority, the ability to "see" God's purpose.

I tell the story in my book, *Spiritual Entrepreneurs*:

> On a chilly but sunny April morning, I went and stood in a field behind the little two-room church building—the site of our current counseling center. Staring back at the modest church facility that looked like hundreds of others, I said: "Lord, I am not going to leave this field until I have a clear sense of your mission for this church."
>
> ... I remained in the field for the rest of the afternoon. And as is so often the case, God speaks, not through storm, fire, or earthquake, but through silence. God's thoughts began to stream into my head. I could see three thousand people worshiping the Lord. A deep sense of God's feeling for the lost overwhelmed me. I am not a highly emotional person, but tears ran down my cheeks as I sensed God's pain for the people who lived thirty minutes in every direction from this location—people who had no understanding of God's love and healing intention.

...I had a vision of a church that would be a teaching church. ...I also saw a church that represented ethnic diversity, where the songs of all cultures were sung and celebrated.

When I left the field it was late afternoon. I left with a sunburn and a clear sense of God's purpose, which has kept me moving forward and sustained me during my ministry.[1]

As I explain in the book, the power of that vision enabled me to see the reality of God's success before it happened. And because I had a clear picture of God's destination, the people began to articulate and live that vision. Over time, that vision began to penetrate the surrounding culture. Vision always clarifies God's purpose and direction.

Too many people quit in the face of resistance and opposition. They never experience the promise of God because they quit stepping forward; they start over again at the beginning.

What opposition or resistance are you facing in your life? Where are you tempted to quit or start over?

_____

_____

You will never reach God's place of promise if you keep starting over. Many people not only do this in their life's work but also in their relationships. I was headed that way when I nearly gave up on my marriage to Carolyn. We were at the twenty-year mark and frustrated by feelings of pain and failure. I am so thankful that we didn't make our decision on the basis of what we were seeing, feeling, and hearing at that moment. We chose instead to focus on what God was intending and creating for our relationship in the future. We began to build daily on the promising picture of God's preferred future. As of this writing we are celebrating more than thirty-five years of marriage and are allowing God to use our lives as a source of health and blessing for others.

Vision Is Nurtured in Community

Vision requires community. The Psalms of Ascent were sung in community. We cannot climb the incline of faith alone. We cannot carry ourselves to the place of wholeness or to the fulfillment of our intended destinies. We need to travel together on this journey, to hear each other's words and stories of faith.

I admire the story in Mark 2:1-11 where the four men carry their paralyzed friend to Jesus. They were faithful, persistent, innovative, and resourceful. That's a rather creative group! Think about the energy it would take to get this one person—dead weight—up onto a roof, and then to cut through the roof to get him down again into the healer's care.

Notice that it took four people to bring this man to Jesus. Have you discovered that you can't get there by yourself? Like the paralyzed man, you need someone to carry you. Carolyn and I would have never made it without others around us to bring us to healing in our relationship.

Some people come to church and say to themselves, "I can hang out by myself, come here, be inspired every weekend, and that's good enough." It's not. You need help to find Jesus through the crowd. You need the faith of your friends when your own faith falters. The paralyzed man was healed *"when Jesus saw their faith"* (verse 5). Whose faith did Jesus see? The faith of the man's friends.

Sometimes I want to ask, "God, where are you?" Do you ever feel that way? I've even found myself occasionally saying, "Is this Jesus thing for real?" We have more faith together than we do by ourselves; sometimes when it's too hard for me to trust God, other people can trust for me.

Who are your traveling companions? Who helps to nurture your vision?

_____

_____

Leland, a ninety-four-year-old friend of mine, helps lower friends through rooftops to be touched by Jesus. "If I sit down at the donut shop and I don't know the person next to me, I strike up a conversation,"

Leland says. "Where do you go to church?" he asks them. If they say they don't go anywhere, Leland takes it as his signal to go after them. "I would say eighteen to twenty have been fetched in by my invitation," Leland reports. He doesn't just invite. He picks them up in his car and brings them to church. "At ninety-four, I won't be around here much longer," he explains, "so I want to cover as much territory in this spiritual aspect as I can. We're told that one of the things we are to do is to be about Jesus' business. So as long as I'm able, I'll be contacting individuals about their spiritual status."

People like Leland get involved. They're resourceful. Since the men could not get their paralyzed friend to Jesus through normal means, they made an opening in the roof above Jesus. In other words, they made doors where there were no doors. After they carved through the roof, can you imagine the mess? I can hear the synagogue people below: "We just put the roof on this building last year!" Jesus didn't die for shingles and nails; he died for paralyzed people who depend on the vision of others to bring them into the community of care and transformation.

Each of us is responsible for developing our own networks of mentoring relationships. Vision is nurtured in community—prophetic communities that bring people to Jesus, people who then grow in authentic relationships and become empowered to serve.

2) Articulate an Attitude of Determined Faith

The tongue is a powerful force that has the potential to bring life or death. "*A word out of your mouth may seem of no account, but it can accomplish nearly anything—or destroy it!*" (James 3:5, THE MESSAGE). Our words emerge from our attitudes to create physical realities. That's why the songs we sing amid the rigors of the journey are songs of celebration, faith, and victory. "*If the LORD had not been on our side . . . / the flood would have engulfed us, the torrent would have swept over us, / the raging waters would have swept us away. / Praise be to the LORD*" (Psalm 124:1, 4-6).

Vision empowers me to sing songs of faith in the face of discouragement and resistance. When you grasp God's vision for your life's work, you celebrate what is right with life. You focus on the positive, redemptive activity of God that is going on continually all around us. When you celebrate what's right, you build vision for God's possibilities and find energy to fix what's wrong!

When you speak, do you tend to celebrate what's right or focus on what's wrong?

_____

_____

We speak faith and hope on the basis of God's promise and not out of the circumstances of the moment. We demonstrate faith in the action of trust. When Peter, crossing the Sea of Galilee in a terrifying storm, heard the voice of Jesus, seemingly coming from an uncertain apparition on the water, he took an irrational risk and stepped out of the boat to attempt the impossible. " 'Lord, if it's you,' Peter replied, 'tell me to come to you on the water' " (Matthew 14:28).

Our verbal attitudes fortify trust. The ancient Jewish pilgrims affirmed that they would trust God regardless of their current circumstances, singing confidence and joy in their Psalms of Ascent: *"Those who trust in the LORD are like Mount Zion, which cannot be shaken but endures forever"* (Psalm 125:1); *"Our mouths were filled with laughter, our tongues with songs of joy"* (Psalm 126:2). Regardless of how the earth moved, vision allowed them to have positive, healthy attitudes. People of vision trust God's promise. They are not heading toward defeat but toward victory, surplus, and abundance.

The Lord is *"on our side,"* affirms Psalm 124:1; and if we look ahead to the back of the book, we know God wins in the end. Jesus died on the cross and rose from the grave. The victory is final. Jesus' salvation is offered to every single person on planet Earth. I might not see the realization of it today; but as long as I am going to die anyway, I am going to sow my life toward God's future.

I keep speaking the promising picture of God's preferred future in spite of the negativity or resistance I might experience in the heat of the moment. As the pilgrims ascending to the Temple long ago sang, *"They have greatly oppressed me from my youth, but they have not gained the victory over me"* (Psalm 129:2). People of vision articulate an attitude of determined faith in all they do.

How can you articulate an attitude of determined faith in the midst of your current circumstances?

_____

_____

3) Initiate Strategic Actions

Vision empowers us to initiate strategic actions that result in a picture of a better future. Without it, we too often reach a plateau and grow discouraged. So often, people suffering from depression and hopelessness are really plagued with a lack of vision. They cannot imagine a positive future or envision a worthy aim to which to devote their lives.

God entrusts vision to those who will faithfully execute it, and the size of vision God gives us is dependent on our faithfulness in implementing strategic action. God wants to do incredible things, but God will not give us a vision that exceeds the size of the faith-steps that we are willing to take.

God has given us everything we need according to God's riches in Christ Jesus our Lord. Vision empowers us to initiate life-changing action, and God will not trust us with a bigger vision than we will implement. God wants to accomplish much on planet Earth but is looking for people who will faithfully act on whatever ideas God places in their minds, in spite of their fear or reservations.

What kind of people is God looking for?

_____ people without fear
_____ people who will act faithfully despite fear

God gives big visions to people who are willing to take big actions! Influence and accomplishment are not about doing the same old things passed along by the managers of sacred traditions that have preceded you. Leadership implements the risky strategic actions necessary to reach God's place of promise. Doers are driven by visions and dreams and not by the expectations or reprisals of people. They are compelled forward by truth, not motivated by the accolades of committees. Leaders do the right thing rather than the expected thing.

A Strategic Action Plan

Every year, I work from a strategic action plan. I get confused by all the business models that present the need for vision statements, mission statements, purpose statements, and highly detailed plans. For me it's simple. I get a clear vision, and I spell out the strategic actions that I will implement this year to get closer to God's place of promise.

This is far more important than a wish list. It is not just an idea ("I'd like to do something big for God"), and it is more than a strategic goal ("I'll need to look into beginning a new worship celebration sometime soon"). It does no good if it is never executed. That is why I work from a yearly strategic action plan. I work and plan as if I have one year to live. This approach allows me to prioritize on the basis of mission-critical-strategic activities. More important, it gives me permission not to do things of less importance.

There are four areas or categories to consider when creating a yearly strategic action plan:

1. Self-Health. If I am not healthy spiritually, emotionally, and physically, then I can't be a source of health and hope to those around me. I place self-health activities into my daily schedule.

2. Relationships. We are created for relationships, and relationships are created in the margins of our lives. I strategically make my family a priority as I plan my strategic direction for each week, month, and year.

3. Work. Our work is not separate from our relationship with God. It is an act of worship. If my work is to continue on the upward ascent as an honorable, excellent offering to God, then I need to be growing in my daily execution. I regularly ask myself: What am I doing this year that is different than what I did last year? It is terribly easy to get stuck in the rut of doing things in the same old ways. If God is always wanting to do new things, we can't put new wine in old wineskins.

4. Mission. God holds each of us accountable for a personal mission outside of our families and workplace. For example, I am currently working with a group of young college and post-graduate students to help them become the radical, excellent Christian leaders of their generation. We meet periodically in different parts of the country for leadership-learning experiences. I assign them regular reading, and I am raising a young hero scholarship fund for any of these young people who pursue graduate work for the purpose of vocational ministry. This personal mission strategy is separate from my home or work commitments.

The K.I.S.S. Principle

The most important thing to remember when creating your own strategic action plan is to follow the K.I.S.S. principle: Keep It Simple Saints. A great strategic plan will focus on a few well-defined and articulated initiatives.

When it came to my one-year strategic action plan for my first year at Ginghamsburg Church, I focused on only three things: 1) preaching a sermon series on the Book of Acts; 2) simplifying the administrative structure to serve Christ's mission rather than the mission of an antiquated structure; and 3) pouring myself into ten strategic leaders who would become the leaders of the movement.

Most people try to do too many things in any one year. Try a different and more effective approach this year. Using the four suggested categories as prompts to your brainstorming, identify three action steps that will keep you focused on mission-critical-strategic activities.

Why is it important to keep it simple when creating a strategic action plan?

_____

_____

Life is too short to live for anything less than a fulfilling, fruitful, faithful purpose. Take time every day to dream God's dream for your life. God gives great vision to those who are willing to take great action!

Momentum Builders

1. What life-picture is God showing you that you would like to begin putting into action? (If you don't have an answer, spend time in prayer this week, asking for a vision of God's purpose and direction for your future.) _____

_____

2. Are you ready to create a strategic action plan for achieving this vision, or do you need to connect with a strategic partner to help you design a plan? If the latter, whom will you ask to help you?

_____

3. Alone or with a partner, write a simple one-year strategic action plan. Review the four areas of self-health, relationships, work, and mission; and prayerfully consider what three action steps will be most strategic and effective in helping you to implement the life-picture God is showing you:

My Strategic Action Plan

1.
2.
3.

[1] Michael Slaughter, *Spiritual Entrepreneurs: Six Principles for Risking Renewal* (Abingdon, 1995); pp. 109–11 (text slightly updated for readability and accuracy).

Week 6
Eating and Exercise for Life

EAT> *To consume as sustenance; to include something as a usual or fundamental part of a diet.*

EXERCISE> *To exert oneself physically or mentally, especially for the purpose of developing or maintaining physical fitness.*

"May the LORD bless you from Zion; may you see the prosperity of Jerusalem all the days of your life. / May you live to see your children's children—peace be on Israel." (Psalm 128:5-6)

Have you ever heard someone make a statement such as "I can't wait to go to heaven" or "I hope that Jesus is coming back soon"? Personally, I can wait! I am in no hurry to make the celestial trip. It's not that I won't be happy to see Jesus—I'm just really enjoying this incredible gift of life.

Sometimes we tend to be like the spoiled child who rips eagerly through the wrapping on Christmas morning but grows bored with the present and discards it by late afternoon. Life is a gift to be embraced and celebrated to the max. I love life's complexities and its intricacies as well as its ordinary joys—from the changing of the seasons to my first cup of coffee in the morning. Even the simple day-to-day routines of life add sparkle to my world—pitching baseballs to my son or hearing my daughter's voice. I love life, and I am in no hurry to let go of this precious gift.

Name some of the everyday and extraordinary things you love about life—things that add sparkle to your world:

_____

_____

The Gift of Life

What makes life unique? The breath of God. *"Then the* LORD *God formed a man from the dust of the ground and breathed into his nostrils the breath of life, and the man became a living being"* (Genesis 2:7). The Hebrew name for Adam sounds like the Hebrew name for dirt. All the elements in a human body can be found in dirt, but you are more than the sum total of chemicals and minerals found in the natural world or elements charted on the periodic table. God breathed Spirit into the human form, adding a sense of mystery to the essence of human life.

That's why every human being matters to God. There are no disposable people. Every human contains the breath of God that brings life. In God's eyes, every single life has value.

I heard actor Christopher Reeve lecture in Philadelphia in the spring of 2004, just a few months before his death. Unable even to move his head, he was totally dependent on a respirator to deliver his breath. His assistant rolled him onto the stage in an elaborate wheelchair. Yet he continued to maximize his gift of life in spite of his overwhelming physical limitations and his life-threatening injuries. He demonstrated that the quality and value of life is not tied to the absence of debilitating injuries or disease. His life gave me fresh appreciation for the breath of God.

As a follower of Jesus Christ, no matter what your ability or disability, your body is the dwelling place of God! *"Do you not know that your bodies are temples of the Holy Spirit, who is in you, whom you have received from God? You are not your own; you were bought with a price. Therefore honor God with your bodies"* (1 Corinthians 6:19-20).

It is tempting for us to dissociate what we eat and whether or not we exercise from our commitments to God, but our bodies are not our own. We have been purchased, body-mind-spirit, with the redemptive work of God through Jesus' life, death, and resurrection. Eating healthy foods and making a disciplined commitment to exercise is not optional for the committed follower of Jesus. It is one of the essential daily life disciplines of discipleship. *"Therefore, I urge you, brothers and sisters, in view of God's mercy, to offer your bodies as a living sacrifice, holy and pleasing to God—this is true worship"* (Romans 12:1). *"Let us purify ourselves from everything that contaminates body and spirit, perfecting holiness out of reverence for God"* (2 Corinthians 7:1).

How is your commitment to God impacting your eating and exercise habits?

_____ **I don't see a connection between my commitment to God and my personal health choices.**

_____ **I see a connection, but I am currently undisciplined in my eating and exercise habits.**

_____ **I recognize that my body is not my own, and I am striving to make some positive changes in my eating and exercise habits.**

_____ **I am honoring God with my body through a disciplined commitment to healthy nutrition and exercise.**

We must honor God in the care of our bodies so we may continue God's work in the excellence of ascent. God intends for the Holy Spirit to operate through our physical bodies. As the body of Christ, we are the hands, feet, and mouth of Jesus on planet Earth for reaching the lost and setting oppressed people free. God needs our bodies to complete the mission of Jesus in the world.

Salvation is a lifestyle of (w)holiness. The purpose of Jesus coming into our lives is not only to save us for heaven, but also to heal us and make us well in every dimension of life so that our bodies can be honorable, excellent offerings to God. Our longevity has value for Jesus' mission!

The Value of Longevity

The Psalms of Ascent place value on longevity. *"May the LORD bless you from Zion; may you see the prosperity of Jerusalem all the days of your life. / May you live to see your children's children—peace be on Israel"* (Psalm 128:5-6).

Your life is a gift from God. You live to serve God's purpose. The fruitful completion of that purpose and the enjoyment of the fruits of your life's labors are both best served by your continued good health.

There is evidence from new research suggesting that long life is the result of disciplined life choices. *Time* magazine's cover article "How to Live to Be 100" says that the dominant factor is lifestyle rather than genetic makeup. "You could have Mercedes-Benz genes," says Dr. Bradley Willcox of the Pacific Health Research Institute in Honolulu, "but if you never change the oil, you are not going to last as long as a Ford Escort that you take good care of."[1] There is no question that a change in eating habits and physical exercise can prolong our lives and foster greater health and vitality into our seventies, eighties, and beyond.

Obesity is one of the leading causes of preventable death in the United States. Being extremely overweight is indisputably lethal, according to the Centers for Disease Control and Prevention.[2] Diet programs abound, but do people stay with them long enough to see lasting benefit? Americans fork over millions in hopes of finding a magic elixir while we continue to pack on the pounds. One calculation says that a third of Americans are not just overweight but obese.[3] Obesity is also reaching epidemic proportions among our children.

Cancer is also linked to our life choices. "Tobacco use, poor diet, and inadequate physical activity combined are related to about 60 percent of all cancer cases, while environmental cancer risks are related to only about 3 percent of cancer cases," reports Dr. J. Nick Baird, director of the Ohio Department of Health.[4] The trouble is that achieving maximum length and quality of life requires hard work and discipline.

What disciplined life choices are you currently making, or are you willing to make, in order to increase your health and longevity?

_____

_____

_____

Factors That Influence Longevity

Would you prefer to stay a bit longer on this earth? Would you like to find greater energy, joy, and fulfillment in this life? Consider these six factors:

1. Attitude: In recent years numerous scientific studies have shown a positive link between faith and longevity.[5] One study, for example, showed that people who pray during illness accelerate their recovery rate.[6]

On the other side, fuming at other drivers or stewing about the boss will shorten your life.[7] Stress has a strong, negative impact on your longevity. It makes your cells deteriorate faster. Its impact shows up on your skin and in your hair. Have you noticed how quickly a new president grays once he occupies the Oval Office? Nutrition and exercise play an important role in the management of stress, but so does your attitude.

2. Relationships: People with healthy relationships tend to live more satisfying lives. Even pets can have a positive impact on the health of those who live alone.

3. Genes: Genetics have some impact on our longevity and health, but a family history of heart disease or cancer doesn't mean we're doomed! Diet can make a difference in the fight against our genetic predispositions. For those of us who are genetically predisposed to prostate cancer, eating more soy, more fresh fruits and certain vegetables, and less saturated fat will decrease the risk.[8] Diet may also have an impact on the genes linked to heart disease, colon cancer, and Alzheimer's.[9]

4. Mental activity: Some parts of the brain will keep growing if they get enough exercise.[10] As we get older, it is important to keep learning new things and trying new activities. Games like crossword puzzles and Sudoku challenge our minds; and frequent reading and discussion of current events help us continue to learn new things, creating new pathways in our brains.

5. Exercise and 6. Diet: The impact of these last two factors on a person's overall well-being cannot be overemphasized. No one wants the debilitation of diabetes; exercise and diet can help keep it at bay. The current number one cause of death in America is heart disease, but it is largely preventable. You can reduce the risk simply by exercising, eating well, and not smoking.

Which of the six factors affecting longevity do you need to address first?

__attitude   __mental activity
__relationships   __exercise
__genes   __diet

Part of my conversion process in the area of health was the realization that loss of momentum can be based in lifestyle. It's why so many people become ineffective in their sixties. They are spiritually, emotionally, and physically tired; so they simply drop off the path of ascent and retire. I don't know about you, but I'm not going to take myself out of God's game because of poor eating and exercise habits.

The Responsibility of Leadership

As I have emphasized throughout this study, all leadership begins with self-leadership, and all of us are leaders in the sense that we have influence on those around us—our children, friends, co-workers, and acquaintances. My influence as a leader comes down to the credibility of my witness to others. Do I demonstrate (w)holiness? Is the lifestyle of Jesus being revealed in my body, mind, and spirit?

It is impossible to lead others effectively if I cannot first lead myself. I must be on the ascent of health holiness if I am to be a healthy, positive, contagious force in the life of others!

It all comes down to commitment to a rigorous daily discipline. This is why we are called disciples. Discipline is painful for the moment in which it is practiced. Many of Jesus' followers left the journey of ascent because they didn't want to pay the ongoing price of discipleship (see John 6:60-66). But those who continue on the incline of discipline will celebrate the blessings of God's promise. *"No discipline seems pleasant at the time, but painful. Later on, however, it produces a harvest of righteousness and peace for those who have been trained by it"* (Hebrews 12:11).

Consider the temptation of Jesus in the wilderness. Satan's first attack was an attempt to get Jesus to submit his mind and spirit to his appetite. After Jesus fasted for forty days, the tempter suggested that Jesus' comfort and relief would come from food. *"If you are the Son of God, tell this stone to become bread"* (Luke 4:3). Jesus had the mental, spiritual, and emotional discipline to turn Satan down. Likewise, your ability to have discipline over your physical body is the doorway to all other disciplines in your life.

King David lost his integrity when he surrendered to his passions. Instead of leading his men in battle—where leaders are supposed to be— he succumbed to his lust for a married woman (see 2 Samuel 11:1-5). Part of what sets humans apart from all other created species is our ability to master physical discipline, to be able to live by the authority of God's Word and the power of the Spirit, not the immediacy of our appetites. Until we are able to exercise discipline over our bodies through the power of the Holy Spirit, our minds and spirits will continue to be held hostage to our appetites and passions.

All leadership begins with self-leadership. You can't lead others until you can lead yourself, including the discipline of managing your physical health so as to lengthen your leadership.

When it comes to your physical health, would you say that you are a leader? Why or why not?

_____

_____

Lengthening Your Leadership

Would you rather be a short-term leader or one who continues to influence others year after year? I had the privilege of attending Asbury Theological Seminary in the 1970s. Julian C. McPheeters, the school's second president, was in his eighties at that time. He was retired but still very active in the seminary community. When you heard him preach, heaven came down! I heard that he learned to water ski in his seventies and that he was still doing aerobic exercise and working with weights in his eighties. He physically outpaced many of us who were still in our twenties! Howard Snyder makes memorable note of this man of God, saying, "Deeply committed to holistic evangelism, McPheeters was instrumental in the integration of nutrition, exercise, physical healing, and social justice, especially racial justice, into the Asbury Seminary curriculum."[11] Dr. McPheeters understood the concept that all leadership begins with self-leadership.

You cannot be a healthy influencer and agent of kingdom change if you are not demonstrating the reality of the kingdom of God within yourself.

Balanced leadership also includes the responsibility of leading children. I have already mentioned the growing crisis of obesity among our kids. This problem can largely be attributed to fast-food dependence, a result of busy lifestyles and single-parent or dual-career households. How many of us as parents turn to McDonald's after a hard day at work because it is cheap and easy? Morgan Spurlock's documentary *Super Size Me* (2004) was a wake-up call for a fast-food-dependent nation. Mr. Spurlock ate nothing but McDonald's food three times a day for one month. His body began a rapid deterioration, exhibiting accelerated weight gain and dangerous increases in liver enzymes.

Fast is easy. Discipline is hard!

Another factor is the way today's children live more sedentary lifestyles. When I was a kid, we played outside. Mom's babysitter was the outdoors, not the television. When you have to play outdoors, you invent things to do. You are active. You are creative. It was a lot healthier than watching television, playing video games, and eating junk food.

If you are not comfortable letting your children play outside unsupervised, find time to go to the park together, get them involved in organized sports, or play catch and take walks together in the evening. Remember, your guidance and leadership involves helping your children learn the importance of physical health in a life of Christian service! Look for ways to take part in physical activities indoors too—pop in a workout video, find fun and challenging exercises and games, or dance together. There are plenty of ways to get started!

We need to take responsibility for our own health by practicing self-leadership to resist foods and habits that limit our potential for lifelong effectiveness.

> **What are some ways you need to practice self-leadership in the area of your health?**
>
> _____
>
> _____
>
> _____

Getting Started

Ready for a life of better eating and exercise? If you are like me, you have no idea where to begin, and you need a conversion-level experience to push you to a point where you actually take meaningful action. My head had listened for years to statements about the importance of healthy eating and exercise. My responses had ranged from "Some day I'll get to it" to "I know a lot of people who are worse off than me."

> **What excuses and rationalizations are you using, or have you used in the past, to avoid making a disciplined commitment to healthy eating and exercise?**
>
> _____
>
> _____
>
> _____

My rationalization proved dangerous. The dinner hour of Friday, August 18, 2000, found me in a Cincinnati restaurant celebrating a family birthday, when I suddenly felt faint. Next thing I remember, paramedics were shoving aspirin into my mouth and rushing me by ambulance to a nearby hospital. After a battery of tests in the next days, my doctor determined that the arrhythmia my heart had exhibited was not an indication of a diseased heart, but rather a huge wake-up call. My 911 experience was the culmination of lifestyle stress, too much caffeine, and a total disregard for physical conditioning in the journey of ascent.

I knew I had to change if I wanted longevity in ministry, future anniversaries to celebrate with Carolyn, and the joy of grandchildren. My conversion had begun!

A few weeks after my heart scare, I shared during a weekend message how I intended to take charge of this neglected area of my life. I forecasted that I would begin a fitness program, but said I needed a trainer to show me how.

Chastity Layne Slone approached me after our final worship celebration and introduced herself as a certified trainer. She told me she would be willing to work with Carolyn and me. We talked about it at home, and a month later set up our first appointment with Chastity. Her first question, as with everyone she trains, was whether we had clearance from our physician. "Filling out a basic health-history evaluation at a fitness club is not enough," she said.

It really helped that we committed as a family to become healthy together. It is a blessing to agree to keep certain unhealthy foods out of the house. It is also encouraging to grow together with your children in this area. All five members of the extended Slaughter family (husband, wife, daughter, son-in-law, son) now work out on a regular basis and have become informed about healthy nutrition practices.

Fitness begins with a change of mind. Why am I willing to sweat and hurt? Because it's not about me. My life is not my own. *"For to me, to live is Christ"* (Philippians 1:21)! What's more, my life patterns will be inherited by the generations that follow me.

Triangle Leg #1: Good Nutrition

I am not particularly fond of the fad diets where you deprive yourself of certain foods for a period of time. Instead, I learned a plan of nutrition that Carolyn and I could practice for life. "Diet changes that really work must be a family decision," says Chastity. "If the family chef tries to offer two kinds of food, you'll reinforce the idea that nutritious food is weird, and it will lead to failure."

Chastity should know. She started her fitness journey long before Carolyn and I wised up. She even competes in body-building events and has won some titles. And she too had an accountability partner in her spouse. "I haven't always felt good about what I eat," she says. "It took an eight-year journey, but I don't crave soda pop the way I used to."

Chastity started at a specific point, as Carolyn and I did, where she determined that her eating and exercise habits would change. She then began to make a long series of firm decisions. "The biggest thing I see with failure is someone who never truly made a mind change," she says. "One of the reasons people give up is that there are so many choices for your food, and that's why the decision to change is so important."

Chastity also notes that people have a higher failure rate if they don't work with a professional who can develop a plan. This could be a certi-fied trainer like her, or perhaps someone with training and passion in exercise science, such as a physical therapist. "Without help from some-one knowledgeable," she says, "you will hit a plateau, and you'll think that's the best you're going to accomplish."

Though Chastity is a trainer who operates her own fitness center, she has emphasized diet just as much as exercise. One of the first questions she asked Carolyn and me was, "What are you eating?" She wanted to help us calculate how many calories we were taking in and what kinds of food we were eating. Some people, such as those who eat irregularly and snack a lot, need to journal in order to determine what they actually take in on a typical day.

In recent years, I've come to follow a healthy, balanced diet that is low in fat, and I have become conscious of my daily intake of carbohy-drates. I'm learning to distinguish the healthier complex carbs from simple carbs that too quickly turn to sugar. I follow the simple rule, "If it's white, it's not right," and opt for whole grains. This includes:

Wild or brown rice over white rice,
Whole-wheat bread over white bread,
Yams over white potatoes, and
Whole-wheat pasta over white pasta.

Vegetables and fruits are a great way to take in healthy carbs, and again I've learned another general rule of thumb: The brighter the color of the fruit and vegetable, the higher the value in vitamins and minerals.

I've started to study food packaging in order to gauge my daily intake of sugar. Many items state in bold letters that they are "0% fat"—but they are loaded with sugar. I have another simple rule: "Don't count daily calories; instead, pay attention to my intake of fats, carbohydrates, and sugar."

I stay away from dessert except on rare, planned occasions.

My eating frequency has also changed. I never used to eat breakfast, but now I realize how important that morning meal is. Breakfast kicks in your metabolism, and it is your metabolism that burns fat.

I now eat three healthy, balanced meals each day; and I supplement these meals with at least two or three smaller healthy snacks. With so many mini-meals, all nutritious, I never feel deprived.

Another Mike maxim: "Stay away from high-fat and high-sugar snack foods." (They will literally kill me!) Almonds and unsalted peanuts are some of my favorite snacks. I will also eat a granola bar or drink a protein supplement for one of my snacks, usually before or after a workout.

Protein is very important for muscle growth. Lean beef, chicken breast, turkey, and fish are excellent sources of protein that are also low in fat. Egg whites and beans are healthy sources for protein. I stay away from fried and breaded foods.

I drink skim milk, and I drink plenty of water every day. For most people, depending on their physician's advice, it is a good idea to supplement their daily diet with a good multivitamin.

If I ever slip in my eating habits, Chastity reminds me that healthy nutrition is 80 percent of the equation in physical fitness. At first, all I could think about was the new foods I didn't especially like or the foods I had to give up. "I can't live without dessert," I'd think.

Then I would remember why I'm making the change: it's not about my likes and food preferences but the mission of the One I serve!

What is one goal you would like to reach in the area of nutrition?

_____

_____

Triangle Leg #2: Aerobic Exercise

Aerobic exercise is intentional physical movement that keeps my heart rate up for twenty to thirty minutes. The focus of aerobic exercise is cardio or heart health.

It is important to do some form of cardio exercise at least three times a week. Many choose to have a daily regimen of walking. This is good. I walk to as many places as possible and avoid elevators in favor of steps whenever possible.

I remember the first time Chastity took me out to run for twenty minutes nonstop. "I've got to stop," I wheezed after just one minute that seemed like ten. "I'm going to die!"

Chastity promised me that it would get better, and it did within a matter of weeks. Today, my aerobic exercise of choice is running three to four times a week on the treadmill. It's easier on my knees and is not affected by the weather.

What is one goal you would like to reach in the area of aerobic exercise?

_____

_____

Triangle Leg #3: Resistance Training

The third part of the fitness triangle is creating resistance with weights. Your muscles are the furnace of your metabolism. Muscle burns fat twenty-four hours a day, seven days a week, even while you sleep. Aerobic exercise burns fat mainly during the time of the exercise, while the heartrate is increased.

I think of it this way: Aerobic exercise makes for heart health while weight training increases physical strength. I try to do three cardio sessions a week and four weight-training sessions. In each of the four weight sessions, I concentrate on different parts of my body. This means I hit each major muscle area once a week.

I am not trying to look like Arnold Schwarzenegger; my goal is to maintain positive momentum for life. On Monday, I concentrate on weight machines and free weights that work my chest and back muscles. On Tuesday morning, I will do a half-hour of cardio exercise on the treadmill. On Wednesday afternoon, I come back to resistance training, concentrating on leg exercises. On Thursday morning, I am back to cardio, running twenty-five to thirty minutes on the treadmill. On Friday morning, I spend twenty-two to twenty-five minutes on the treadmill in my basement and then hit the gym on the way home from the office in order to work my shoulder muscles (thus a double session on Friday). On Saturday morning I am back at the gym to work my triceps and biceps. Sunday is my day of rest.

Notice that I do three cardio and four weight training sessions that target all of my major muscle groups. The best way to learn to exercise with a safe, healthy routine is to become part of a gym or exercise facility where they have classes and trainers who know what they are doing and can teach you to use the right form that will minimize the possibility of injury and maximize the effectiveness of your time spent in the gym.

Remember, good nutrition is 80 percent of the key to your desired results because food is the fuel that runs the car. Our bodies were not designed to run on inferior fuel!

What is one goal you would like to reach in the area of resistance training?

_____

_____

Just as all leadership begins with self-leadership, all excellence—including our ability to influence people positively—begins there too.

Our bodies are not our own. We are called to honor God with them. Until we exercise discipline over our bodies, our minds and spirits will be held hostage to our passions and appetites.

Your life is a gift; your body is God's temple. Make your life and body an honorable, excellent offering to God through the discipline of healthy eating and exercise.

Momentum Builders

1. Meditate on 1 Corinthians 6:19-20. What is God saying to you?

   _____

   _____

2. Recall the factor affecting longevity that you identified as your top priority (p. 94). What is one thing you need to do related to this factor?

   _____

   _____

3. All leadership begins with self-leadership. Name some positive and negative ways you have influenced the people closest to you in regard to healthy lifestyle issues:

   Positive Influences   **Negative Influences**

4. Review the excuses and rationalizations you listed on page 97. Which one seems to carry the most weight? Write it below. Then ask the Holy Spirit to help you identify the deception underlying this excuse, as well as the truth pertaining to it. Here is one example:

   Excuse/Rationalization: *Some day I'll start to take better care of myself.*
   Underlying Deception: *I can wait to take care of my physical body.*
   Truth: *I don't know what tomorrow will bring.*

Excuse/Rationalization: _____

Underlying Deception: _____

Truth: _____

5. Review the goals you set for the three "triangle legs" of good health (pp. 101–02) and write at least one step you will take to achieve each goal:

   Nutrition: _____

   _____

   Aerobic Exercise: _____

   _____

   Resistance Training: _____

   _____

[1] Richard Corliss and Michael D. Lemonick, "How to Live to Be 100," *Time*, August 30, 2004; p. 103.

[2] "New Calculation: Obesity Now No. 7 Among Causes of Death," April 5, 2005, www.cnn.com/2005/HEALTH/diet.fitness/04/20/obesity.deaths.ap/index.html.

[3] Michael D. Lemonick, "The Year of Obesity," *Time*, December 27, 2004.

[4] "Cancer linked to choices," *Dayton Daily News*, December 2, 2004.

[5] Kenneth H. Cooper, *Faith-Based Fitness* (Nelson, 1995); pp. 3–10.

[6] Cooper, *Faith-Based*; pp. 3–10.

[7] Corliss and Lemonick; p. 103.

[8] "Health for Life," *Newsweek*, January 17, 2005; p. 48.

[9] "Health for Life," *Newsweek*, January 17, 2005; p. 48.

[10] "Health for Life," *Newsweek*, January 17, 2005; p. 61.

[11] Howard A. Snyder, "Holiness in Post Modernity: Holiness and the Five Calls of God," paper presented to the Asbury Theological Seminary community on November 11, 2004.